To Jan
Aug 1946
from — Al

PAINTING AND PAINTERS

LIONELLO VENTURI

PAINTING
AND
PAINTERS

HOW TO LOOK AT A PICTURE

FROM GIOTTO TO CHAGALL

560659

CHARLES SCRIBNER'S SONS

NEW YORK · MCMXLV

$\mathcal{F}$oreword

BOOTH TARKINGTON

IN THIS BOOK Dr. Lionello Venturi explains how we can and should look at pictures in the manner he believes will best profit us. When anybody offers to tell us how to do anything, we're naturally interested in the quality of his competence. Before we accept advice we want to know who and how fit is the adviser. Probably most of the people who read Dr. Venturi's book will already know much of him; but for the others it may be reassuring to examine for a moment the rather staggering list of his equipments. We can do no more than glance at them; an elaborated record would necessitate a Foreword so long that there'd be little room in the book for what Dr. Venturi himself has to say.

At the age of twenty-two he had his Ph.D. from the University of Rome. At the age of twenty-four he was Vice-Director of the Academy of Art in Venice and of the Borghese Gallery in Rome, precociously acquired dignities that must have been gratifying to his illustrious father, the universally revered scholar, pre-eminent Italian historian of art, Adolfo Venturi. Relationship between father and son was always as close intellectually as it was in affection.

Lionello Venturi was Director of the National Gallery in Urbino before he was thirty; then for seventeen years he was Professor of History of Art in the University of Turin, where he formed the famous Gualino Collection now the property of the Italian State. In 1940 he was Visiting Professor at Johns Hopkins; 1941, Visiting Professor at the University of California; 1942, Visiting Professor at the University of Mexico City; 1943, École Libre des Hautes Études in New York. He has been a contributor to an imposing number of the authoritative magazines of art, a lecturer at the Sorbonne, at Lyons University, at London University, at the Fogg Art Museum, at Yale, at Smith, at Columbia, etc. His published books run up to about twenty and indicate the almost startling variety of his interests and researches. He has written elaborately upon Giorgione, upon Leonardo, upon Botticelli — and upon Pissarro, Cézanne, and Rouault. His most recent books have been *Art Criticism Now,* 1941, and *Peintres Modernes,* 1942.

We admit immediately that a man of these experiences and proficiences couldn't easily fail to have something to say to us and that when he tells us how he thinks we should look at pictures we shall have the benefit of a background as enriched as capacious. We may agree with him or disagree; nevertheless, he possesses the right to have weight with us. He will not instruct us offhand or impulsively. What he says will have premeditation, large informations, behind it.

One cheerful egoist might ask, "Why do I want anybody to tell me how to look at pictures?" Another might inquire, "Why *need* I be told how to look at them?" The answer to both is as simple as "Two heads are better than one." If the second head is better than the first, then the first may become more than doubly wise by absorbing what's in the second. If one of the heads is wrong-headed, the other will have strengthened its rightness in the exercise of setting the wrong head right. It's quite possible that some readers will quarrel with Dr. Venturi's exposition. Even so they will not be losers by reading his book. They will have gained handsomely by the comprehension of a point of view opposite to their own. We cannot intelligently quarrel with what we do not understand.

In how many ways are pictures usually observed? Probably in about as many ways as there are ways for individual dispositions to follow their own idiosyncratic likings and dislikings. On this point Dr. Venturi in his Introduction says a primary sort of thing useful to remember: ". . . It is not true that any one can judge a work of art by just listening to the inner voice of his naked soul."

This seems to me an interesting way of saying that the art-talker who "knows what he likes" knows only something about himself, and when he praises what he likes, slighting or mocking what he doesn't, he sets up to be a critic but is unimportant, except perhaps to his mother, because he is merely autobiographical.

Of course I mustn't devote these few pages to paraphrasing or interpreting Dr. Venturi to the reader; I'm only the "Announcer." Nevertheless, I take it to be a part of the privilege of becoming such a herald to use Dr. Venturi's warning about our naked souls as a text incentive to a little discursiveness. Thus, elaborating, I seem to perceive that a stark-naked soul has nothing but its naked likes and dislikes — nothing much better than its artlessness — and bare naïveté is no more trustworthy in a gallery of paintings than in a chemist's laboratory. In either the gallery or the laboratory, ignorance can blow itself up; and a complacent slight knowledge, too, can be disastrous. Sorcerers' Apprentices uncork horrible turbulences.

This doesn't mean that only a rarefied culture should dare to look at pictures or take pleasure in them. Nothing more sinister is intended than the inference that our opinions upon works of art, as upon anything else, need all the foundations we can put under them, or they are likely not to be worth expressing or even possessing. Moreover, when we rise above our likes and dislikes to form what we believe to be dispassionate judgments, these can be tricky. Sometimes we're confident that they're solidities, sound for the ages — and presently they prove as sly as quicksilver. Most often they are not ours at all, never were; we've only caught them like colds. Again, with a little time or a change of place, we see them as shameful ghosts we're mortified to have consorted with.

Lately I looked at a lithograph entitled *Joan of Arc,* done probably in the 'eighties of the last century. Joan is shown advancing her oriflamme, her long black hair afloat upon the wind, oval face pretty and romantically inspired, body armored from graceful neck to opulent thigh but large of bust, tiny of waist under the accommodating steel. She has as thoroughly the hour-glass figure as has any corset advertisement or Black Crook poster of the time of the lithograph. Nowadays nobody needs to withhold laughter; every one knows that Joan didn't look like that or dress like that. Nevertheless, when this picture was made only a few crotchety students would have said, "Nonsense!"

The foolish thing's general acceptance came of course because of the special fashion of that day, which jammed the

viii

female figure into extremities of the hour-glass shape. The pretty face fancied to be Joan's, the big black eyes and the romantic hair were then the proper accessories; but the hour-glass for bust, waist, and hips was a necessity — the 'eighties couldn't have believed in a Joan who was otherwise. Even in armor the Maid, centuries dead, had to be 1880-stylish or the lithographer couldn't have drawn what he thought was a picture of her. Neither he nor "his public" were archæologists; they hadn't the power to imagine an attractively heroic girl who wasn't hour-glassed; Greek waists were unattractive.

There's of course no implication here that the hour-glass figure can't appear in a work of art, anachronistically or not; I am only pointing out that in this lithograph we all plainly see now a particular thing virtually invisible to the people of the 'eighties although it was close before their eyes. We see a ludicrously impossible figure; they saw something they believed to be Joan of Arc.

We know that no man can escape from his own period — willy-nilly he must be of it, chained down to it — but he has at least the power to free himself from the pressure of his haberdasher. He can even go further and keep clear vision when this decade's styles in painting and sculpture are shown at fashionable exhibitions of art. He can't fly out of his period; but he can avoid being harnessed in blinders by any of the series of fashions that succeed one another before his eyes.

When the fashionable way of looking at things has full hold upon us we're victims of the flitting hour. The next hour most certainly arrives and forefronters deride what they thought valuable an hour agone. Life is as befuddled as this for minds fluffy enough to float on the fashions; but no person capable of meditative thought upon his own education needs to be that fluffy.

The meditative thought would not be enough without the education, and the education might easily be frazzled without the meditation. Current styles in seeing and thinking — even current styles in emotion — are insidiously contagious, especially so, of course, for enthusiastic natures. Current styles may be "good" styles and yet be as blinding as "bad" ones. The merely stylish person, his vision slave to his modishness, utters the loud and vacant laugh of contemptuous sophistication when his led eyes behold the styles that yesterday enthralled him or his father. For the stylish of today, only today's style, and styles somewhat like it in the past, are "good" ones.

Thus stylishness is a kind of provincialism or localization in time, and the more "correct" the up-to-dateness of the victim, the more surely is he to be a joke on the morrow. The paintings that Father bought go up to the garret as Grandfather's come down. Some day Father's will come down, too. Then perhaps both will go up again, or to the auction block, making room for brighter canvases of the hurriedly passing present — these to be banished laughingly with the coming of a newer hour of illusion.

How may we live free of the continuously changing series of small illusions? How may we learn at least to see with the eyes of our whole period, and not with glaucoma gaze directed, as through gun-barrels, at tiny areas bright one moment, dark the next, and forever sliding out of sight? For the development of those necessities, education and meditation, we need all the educative and meditative aid that's offered. Out of the history of man some truths about him have emerged into the light, and out of the history of art more than mere changing appearances may be discerned in that same illumination. For those who seek clarities, this book of Dr. Venturi's can be of high advantage.

Author's Note

I HERE acknowledge my indebtedness to my dear friend, the late Dino Ferrari, who dedicated to the editorial work on this book his intelligence and whole-hearted devotion.

I wish to thank the following for the use of their photographs: Alinari, Florence, for Figures 1 and 20; Anderson, Rome, for Figures 2, 5, 6, 7, 9, 11, 13, 15, 17, 19, 24, 25; Reali, Florence, for Figure 3; Uffizi, Florence, for Figure 4; Yale University for Figure 8; Giraudon, Paris, for Figures 10 and 21; Braun, Paris, for Figure 14; Hanfstaengl, Munich, for Figures 18 and 23; Bulloz, Paris, for Figures 22 and 33; the Archives Photographiques, Paris, for Figures 27 and 28; Durand-Ruel, New York, for Figures 35, 37, and 43; the Municipal Museum of Amsterdam for Figure 36; the Museum of Modern Art for Figures 39 and 44; Bernheim Jeune, Paris, for Figure 41; the Metropolitan Museum of Art for Figure 42; Pierre Matisse, New York, for Figures 45, 51, and 53; the Photographic Association of Berlin for Figure 47; Paul Rosenberg, New York, for Figures 48, 49, and 50; Alfred Stieglitz, New York, for Figure 52.

LIONELLO VENTURI

Contents

Plates

xvii

PLATES

Between pages 78 and 79

Fig. 15. GIORGIONE: *The Thunderstorm,* c. 1505.
Gallery, Venice.

Fig. 16. TITIAN: *The Temptation of Adam and Eve,* 1565–70.
Prado, Madrid.

Fig. 17. MICHELANGELO: *The Temptation of Adam and Eve,* 1508–10.
Sistine Chapel, The Vatican.

Fig. 18. TITIAN: *Christ Crowned with Thorns,* 1570–71.
Gallery, Munich.

Fig. 19. EL GRECO: *The Pentecost,* c. 1606.
Prado, Madrid.

Between pages 98 and 99

Fig. 20. CARAVAGGIO: *The Call of St. Matthew,* c. 1592.
San Luigi dei Francesi, Rome.

Fig. 21. REMBRANDT: *The Supper in Emmaus,* 1648.
Louvre, Paris.

Fig. 22. REMBRANDT: *Portrait of Himself,* c. 1663.
Lord Iveagh Collection, London.

Fig. 23. TITIAN: *Portrait of Jacopo da Strada,* 1568.
Museum, Vienna.

Fig. 24. RAPHAEL: *Portrait of a Cardinal,* c. 1511.
Prado, Madrid.

Fig. 25. VELASQUEZ: *The Child of Vallecas* (Detail), c. 1656.
Prado, Madrid.

Between pages 116 and 117

Fig. 26. GOYA: *The Execution of the Third of May,* painted in 1814.
Prado, Madrid.

Fig. 27. MILLET: *The Angelus,* 1859.
Louvre, Paris.

Fig. 28. MEISSONIER: *1814,* painted in 1864.
Louvre, Paris.

Fig. 29. COURBET: *Stone-Breakers,* 1849.
Gallery, Dresden.

Fig. 30. TOULOUSE-LAUTREC: *À la Mie,* 1891.
Bernheim Jeune, Paris. (With a photograph of the models.)

xviii

PLATES

PLATES

Between pages 198 *and* 199

PAINTING AND PAINTERS

Introduction

WHEN LOOKING at a painting, you may be indifferent to it; but if you are moved at all by it you either say: "I like it," or "I don't like it." And you are neither right nor wrong, because individual preferences are beyond discussion. If you like a girl that I do not, it would be stupid or even worse for me to interfere and try to convince you that you must not like her. Individual preference is always arbitrary.

In forming a judgment on art, individual preference cannot be avoided. A "nice girl" by Renoir will appeal more to many people than a rough peasant by Cézanne. But many people, in spite of their preference for Renoir, will admit not only that the rough peasant by Cézanne deserves attention, but also that there is something in the picture of the peasant that is not in Renoir's painting. At this point, you become aware that the qualities of two paintings can be different: one more appealing, the other less so. Nevertheless each has its quality. The quality of a work of art therefore is not completely dependent upon its having an appeal to you, since it is a quality pertaining to the painting itself, and not to your liking or disliking. It is an objective quality, a quality itself. And this quality is called *art*.

Then you as the hypothetical spectator will think or say: "I like Renoir's nice girl very much more than I like Cézanne's rough peasant, yet I recognize that both have that quality which makes them works of art." At this point, one

1

ceases to indulge in an arbitrary preference, and enters the field of art criticism. The statement, "this is a work of art"; or the statement, "this is not a work of art," is the first and ultimate conclusion of art criticism.

The expression of an individual preference or such a conclusion of art criticism has each a different character. As already stated, an individual preference is always arbitrary. Therefore it is never right, but, also, never wrong. A critical conclusion, on the contrary, must be either right or wrong, because it is based on the objective quality of a work — on the statement that it is a work of art — or on the contrary that it is not a work of art. Not all statements can be proved by reasoning, but all must be supported by some evidence, without which they are false statements.

In order to proceed from the first impression of one's individual preference for a work of art to the objective statement of art criticism, the first requisite is culture. Therefore it is not true that any one can judge a work of art just by listening to the inner voice of his naked soul. What is true is that without artistic sensibility no artistic judgment is possible. Artistic sensibility, however, is not as simple a thing as an electron, but a composite of many human activities. It is common knowledge that those people who like to look at paintings, and have looked at many of them and continually look at them, are better able to judge a painting, be it good or bad, than people who lack that knowledge. And those who have had the patience to compare their own judgments with those of other people, trying to understand why they must agree or disagree — these patient students have taken a farther step in enriching their sensibilities. Moreover, since

2

life and nature are always more or less represented in a painting, those people who have a broad experience of life and nature are much better equipped to understand what art is. And finally, the form of sensibility itself is always vague, so that when its contours become definite, sensibility becomes transformed into ideas. Then new impulses of sensibility spread beyond these ideas, giving rise to new ideas, and so on without end. Without ideas, sensibility cannot be developed and refined, but no artistic judgment is possible with ideas alone. The interaction of both sensibility and ideas is essential to artistic culture.

Artistic culture can attain a good understanding of art only when there is a balance between sensibility and ideas. When sensibility predominates, the understanding remains vague and incoherent, because it is subject to the impulses of the moment. Then the contingent prevails over the eternal. When ideas prevail and sensibility is subordinated to rules that are too rigid, what is lost is the sight of reality itself.

Everything in life has the virtue of its defects, and vice versa. Examples of the benefits and shortcomings of different types of artistic culture are the following: Think of a man who walks through a museum and has a good memory for the names and the dates of the artists there represented. He will be proud of his erudition, will stick to it, and probably will want to teach it to every one he meets. His erudition will no doubt be spectacular. Many will admire it. But by memory alone no artistic consciousness will evolve from it. He will tell you that Raphael was born in 1483, in the wonder town of Urbino, where a soldier of fortune, Federico da Montefeltro, had built up one of the most beautiful palaces of the Renais-

3

sance and filled it with wonderful paintings and sculptures, together with a library that was considered the best one at that time in the world. That little town, which until then had been scarcely more than a modest village, shortly became a great center of culture. There Raphael found the opportunities that led him to the great center of painting, Florence; and then to Rome, where, because of Raphael's own creations, artists have gone in pilgrimage for centuries. So when Raphael died at only thirty-seven years of age, everybody mourned him not only as the greatest painter of Christianity, but as a demigod presented by the Almighty to the City of Rome in order to reveal the supernal values of beauty. All this is undoubtedly interesting as a legend, howsoever based on historical facts, but it will be of very little help in understanding a painting by Raphael. In fact, it may even confuse the real quality of the painting with an extraneous halo, which is nothing but historical rhetoric.

Another visitor to the museum will be a lady, for example, who may have read many poems and novels, but having no critical attitude to speak of, enjoyed those poems and novels by falling in love with the protagonists or by hating them. She will see in the museum figures of medieval knights or of modern heroes of revolutions, of dignified princes or of poor peasants in their hut. Her imagination will build up a story around the figures she has seen, and she will believe she likes the figures themselves. But what she will actually like are the stories suggested by the figures. Walter Scott or Victor Hugo, Kipling or Zola, will, in the memory of the lady, substitute his own imagination for the painter's work. This literary type of culture is certainly helpful in

4

looking at a painting, but must be regarded critically — instead of veiling it with extraneous imaginings — in order to reveal the intimate, particular quality of any one painting. Otherwise, it is apt to color our judgment of any work of art with fanciful elaborations that have nothing to do with the work in question.

Another visitor to the museum will say: "When I look at a painting I don't care to know its author, his feeling, his history. The only thing I care for is to enjoy the painting before me. I have a sense of beauty, and by this sense I can judge whether a painting is beautiful or ugly, without bothering with further enquiry." This visitor has indeed a sense of beauty. But if we ask him, "What is beauty?" he will fail to answer. Or he will answer with nonsense. In fact, it must be pointed out here that many artists, as well as many philosophers, have tried throughout the centuries to answer this simple question, and they all failed. So we must admit that this suggests that the question is unanswerable, and it *is* unanswerable because it is a wrong question. Moreover, we can plainly state that beauty, as a thing in itself, does not exist. What is beauty for Homer is not beauty for Shakespeare, what it is for Raphael it is not for Cézanne or Van Gogh. Every artist worthy of his name has an individual conception of beauty and identifies his conception of it with his own imagination; so that to appreciate his sense of beauty we have only to understand his imagination, without having to establish a relationship between his imagination (which reveals itself in his work) and something which we call beauty (which we do not know where to find).

But the visitor might insist: "Forget the work of art for

the time being and think of nature, instead. There is a beautiful woman, and there is an ugly one. How do you explain the difference?" Once a queen asked a poet whether a lady he spoke of was beautiful. The poet answered: "Worse than that." He meant that there was in the lady a vitality which compelled him to stop day-dreaming over ideal beauty and come down to earth, to actual life, with all the excitement, enthusiasm and evil which life entails. True, actual life may be worse but it is more than beauty. What we call beauty in a woman is only her power of life and enchantment, something she creates when she wants to. She is her own artist, and her beauty must be identified with her personality.

But an impersonal sunset is sometimes beautiful, too. A peasant preoccupied with the herding of his cattle, or a millionaire preoccupied with the sixty-miles speed of his car, will not be aware of the beauty of a sunset. On the other hand, the Italian poet, Dante, before a sunset, imagined the loneliness of a mariner far from his home; Eilshemius imagined a great flame burning the sky to death. That is, the beauty of a sunset is nothing else than the imaginary and sentimental reaction to it of the beholder, a reaction due to what we call our sense of beauty, and which is nothing really but our artistic sense. To this reaction Dante gave a poetic realization; Eilshemius a pictorial one. The natural sunset is therefore only a pretext for a work of art, which we and the artist realize as we can.

It is true that people generally believe that some sunsets are beautiful in themselves. But very few are aware that a simple leaf, fallen in autumn from a tree, can also be beautiful. The leaf may stir the imagination of a poet or painter.

6

INTRODUCTION

Many poets and painters understand, and have always understood, the power of suggestion that a simple leaf may have on their imagination. There is no difference between a glorious sunset and a humble leaf. Both appear as things of beauty when some one has artistic sense enough to depict or describe them as beautiful.

The culture of beauty, either by reasoning on what is beautiful, or by searching in any painting for what we believe is beautiful, is certainly useful in essaying a work of art, but only on condition that it does not distract from looking at the painting as an accomplishment in itself. Otherwise we might believe that a poor painting is a masterpiece because it represents a beautiful object; or a masterpiece is rubbish because it represents a common object.

Another way largely recommended for the understanding of painting is the actual practice of painting. It is without any doubt one of the best ways, but not because of the reasons generally attributed to it. If our artistic sensibility comes in contact with nature; if we portray a leaf or a tree, a man or an animal; if through the actual process of painting we study the relation between figure and space, between surface and depth, line and plasticity, color and light—and not only that, but if we can also perceive the intimate correspondence between the life of the subject and its surroundings, and the theoretical or moral consequences of that correspondence— then we shall be able to acquire a perfectly trained imagination capable of comparing our own reaction to nature with the reaction of all artists present and past. If we now ponder what this training means, we shall soon be aware that it is, above all, experience of life, of vision, feeling, imagining, thinking, and willing. And experience in life is the best school for the understanding of art as well as for the understanding of all human achievements.

But when people advise a young man to learn painting in order to understand it, they mean that all he needs to learn is technique, the use of color in oil or tempera, objective or photographic drawing, proportions, anatomy, perspective, balance in composition, etc. Of course, all this knowledge is useful, because it belongs to human experience. And nothing which pertains to human experience ought to be discarded. But a knowledge of technique alone can be very dangerous, hampering the understanding of art. Every now and then we hear the impressions of physicians, who are often art lovers, on painting. They know anatomy very well indeed. And who should know it better than they! Hence a painting which disregards anatomy is an ugly painting to them. Generally speaking, people who have made the effort to learn a certain technique, do not very easily forego the privilege of taking their knowledge as a standard of judgment. They cling to such knowledge, right or wrong, very tenaciously. But there is no such a thing as *the* technique of painting. There are many — the number is almost infinite — techniques of painting. If the painter who painted the picture in the museum happens to have employed the same type of technique as the visitor who learned how to paint, the visitor will readily understand him. But if he has used a different technique, the visitor is apt to think the difference in technique a mistake in technique, and he may remain blind to the really artistic quality of the painting.

The types of people who look at paintings in museums

in these ways might be multiplied *ad infinitum*. Their culture, even if useful to their understanding of art, will not be sufficient until they have formulated a principle of art criticism, and a method for applying their principle. Moreover, the method of criticism changes in accordance with the culture and the temperament of the critic. But certain types of method may be singled out here to clarify this point in our discussion.

There used to be in vogue an old system of criticism which was based on the classic principle that painting is like poetry. A poem has subject matter, and, according to this old system, so has a painting. Thus art criticism began to consider subject matter and to analyze it as though it were narrated in a poem. Form and color were considered only as means to express subject matter. This was the system of classic criticism. The fault of this system was that it held in too high appreciation many paintings that had no artistic value whatsoever, simply because they represented subject matters of interest to a critic's own feeling. If the critic was full of moral and patriotic enthusiasm, he praised the great deeds of Greeks, Romans and medieval knights, or any historical event which distracted him from the artist's forms and colors, and imagination. The critic substituted his own imagination for that of the artist, thus, wittingly or unwittingly, creating a new work of art himself.

The system of criticism prevailing in our time refuses to accept the artistic value of subject matter, and further discards any psychological interference, in order to reduce a painting to its essential visual elements. Recently, during a congress on æsthetics, a program calling for the application of scientific method to art criticism was seriously advocated. The scientist who sponsored this program said that during the Middle Ages certain treatises on zoology titled Bestiaries defined the lion as a noble being, the fox as an astute one, and so on. But today physiology speaks of the structure of the lion and not of his nobility. The same reform, the scientist continued, must be brought to criticism. Instead of values, it must speak of structure. That may be useful for science. But if we followed the scientist's thesis, we should build up a criticism of beasts and not of painting, poetry, or music. What matters in painting is not the canvas, the hue of oil or tempera, the anatomical structure, and all other measurable items, but its human contribution to our life, its suggestions to our sensations, feeling and imagination.

Fortunately, however, there is still a third system of criticism, which, we believe, is more consonant with sound principles of æsthetics and with art itself, and which it is the purpose of this book to illustrate in the following chapters while examining concrete works of art.

It is based on a distinction between subject matter and content, and on the unity of content and form. Suppose a painter wishing to represent the Madonna and Child paints a woman and a child he loves. The subject matter will be the Madonna and Child, but the content of the painting really is the painter's love. Another painter, representing a Madonna and Child, emphasizes his devotion by stressing the character of God and His Mother. The subject matter would be the same as that of the previous picture (Madonna and Child), but the content of the two paintings will be very different — the content of the former being love, and that of

the latter devotion. The subject matter is *what* the painter
has reproduced; the content is *how* the painter has conceived
his subject matter. When one speaks of *how* he conceived
something, he really speaks of *form*. Thus content and form
are identified.

Now consider what many people call form in painting,
that is line, plasticity, color. Modern criticism tries to judge
these by themselves, praising the strongly plastic, the balanced, the subordination of colors to relief, etc. However,
above all, it must be pointed out here that none of these
purely visual facts are values in themselves. Plastic values do
not exist. What exists is a relation between plasticity and
the imagination of the painter who creates plasticity. If the
created plasticity corresponds to the painter's imagination,
this means that his imagination has been realized in plasticity.
Plasticity, like all other types of visualizing, is a symbol of
a value which must be found in the painter's own imagination. An artist's imagination is not an abstraction living in
a vacuum outside his mind. Among other things, it may
also contain the love or the devotion which constitutes the
content of a painter depicting a Madonna and Child, as
already mentioned. Imagination does not work in a void;
it works in the whole life of the artist, and it is the form of
the artist's life. Thus the particular visualizing which is the
characteristic style of an artist, is also the physical symbol
of that artist's imagination.

To detach the subject matter, the content, or the physical
elements of form, line, plasticity, and color from the whole
of a painting, means to destroy the work of art. The unity
of all these elements, in one harmonious fusion, means ar-

tistic life; their separation is, for all elements, artistic death.

Subject matter can have an intellectual, moral, or economic value, but not artistic value until it has been absorbed and transformed by the imagination of the artist. A content can have a sentimental value, but it has no artistic value until the artist's imagination realizes it in an individual form. A line, a plasticity, a harmony of colors, has only technical value, until the artist's imagination impresses it with his passion, with his individual content.

The system of criticism illustrated in the following pages ignores, therefore, any standard of judgment outside the personality of the artist. This does not mean that it ignores any objective standard. The personality of the artist is objective if we know how to interpret and understand him, if we penetrate into his state of mind, follow his process of creation, the struggle of his imagination with his ideas, his moral sense, and his technique in order to reach his unity of form and content. If his free imagination overwhelms his ideologic purposes, his bowing to fixed laws, his learned technique, then he is an artist and his result will be a work of art. Otherwise, he will be a theorist, a propagandist, an artisan — all useful people indeed. But everybody knows or should know, that they must be distinguished from the artist, if the word *art* is to have any meaning.

All methods, even the best ones, involve certain dangers. Indeed, if we study a painting with the aim of reconstructing the personality of the artist, we run the risk of appreciating what is psychologically interesting in his process of creation more than the result of his work. In other words, we run the risk of concentrating on his artistry rather than on his

12

work of art. But this danger can be avoided by recognizing it. The personality of the artist is different from the personality of the man. The man, with all his passions, theories, and duties, motivates and participates in the personality of the artist, but cannot be identified with it. Only when he lets his imagination go beyond all the materials he disposes of, and subordinates his theories, passions, duties and practical interests to the freedom of his imagination — thus identifying his content and his form — then only will his personality appear as that of an artist and not that of a scientist, a moralist, a technician, or a sentimental man.

This principle of the unity of content and form makes the critic stick to the work of art, and not to artistry. Every painting that is not a work of art was made for some purpose outside the field of art, either scientific or moral, either economic or passional. Therefore when you look at a picture, let the analysis of its scientific, moral, or passional peculiarities work as a reagent and by contrast orient you as a critic, until you possess a clear consciousness of what kind of artistic personality you have before your eyes.

Chapter One

GOD AND MAN

EVERY PAINTING is a statement presenting the spectator with a reality involving both matter and mind.

In figure 1, *Joaquin and the Shepherds* by Giotto, the picture includes three men, a little dog, some small sheep, a sheepfold, a rocky mountain sprigged with rare trees, and the sky. To see such ordinary things in the country is not very difficult and nobody would trouble himself to take a trip to Padua to see some men, some sheep, and a dog. Yet the trip has been taken many times by art lovers because they wanted to know just how Giotto imagined the scenes he painted and how he represented the reality he perceived. What they searched for was not the actuality of men and sheep, but the more profound reality of Giotto's painting.

To understand Giotto's reality we must first discard prejudice. It is easy to see that the proportion between the sheep and the men, or the rocks and the men, is different from what we experience in nature. But to believe that Giotto—

Fig. 1. GIOTTO: *Joaquin and the Shepherds*, c. 1305.

Fig. 2. GIOTTO: *Head of Christ*, c. 1305.

Fig. 3. ANONYMOUS MASTER: *Head of Christ*, c. 1290.

Fig. 4. BONAVENTURA BERLINGHIERI: *St. Francis*, 1235.

Fig. 5. SIMONE MARTINI: *Annunciation*, 1333.

who for six centuries has been considered one of the greatest masters of painting — could not see the proportion of things in nature, as does the average man of today, would be a serious lack of understanding. Such a prejudice is rooted in the concept that art is an imitation of nature, a very old opinion, but now thoroughly discredited, because we have improved our consciousness of what constitutes art.

Today the easiest refutation of the theory of art as an imitation of nature is photography; for a photograph usually reproduces nature mechanically. But such a photograph cannot be considered a work of art. When certain photographers motivated by a genuine artistic impulse became aware of this difference they managed to modify their work in order to distinguish it from the simple reproduction of nature. And in so far as they succeeded in representing a personal vision of the world, they attained the artistic level. As a result the vision of nature held by the average photographer and that held by the "pictorial photographer," as the latter has been called, developed into two different categories. They were, and are, different in quality, because the vision of the average photographer is that of an artisan, and the vision of the "pictorial photographer" is that of an artist.

When everybody believed that painting was an imitation of nature, a legend was created about Giotto. In his boyhood Giotto was a poor shepherd who enjoyed himself by drawing on stones the sheep he guarded. According to this legend, Cimabue, a renowned painter, was walking through the countryside, saw one of Giotto's drawings, and, perceiving at once his talent for painting, became his teacher, until the pupil surpassed the master. This legend, of course, has no historical basis in fact, but it is in itself a charming bit of art, because it transforms into a human comedy the impression that Giotto put reality into his paintings, and did so with more popular feeling than Cimabue did.

If, however, we take the legend for granted and look at the sheep in figure 1, we must conclude that his portrayal of sheep was unsuccessful, both as a shepherd boy and as a mature painter. But really to understand Giotto we must forget the legend, ignore the theory of art as being an imitation of nature, and try to grasp *why* he portrayed men and sheep in his picture as he did.

Giotto created a great revolution in painting; but no revolution completely cuts itself off from tradition; and he, too, remained faithful to some principles of his tradition.

Figure 4 represents an image of St. Francis between two angels, and six episodes in the Saint's life. This painting is by Bonaventura Berlinghieri and is dated 1235. Giotto's painting is dated about 1305. Seventy years had elapsed between the two and many changes in taste had occurred, but one principle remained firm — the proportion of things did not depend on their mere appearance in nature, but on their importance in human thought; they were hierarchical proportions. What Berlinghieri wanted to represent was the majesty of the figure of the Saint, his holy majesty; the angels and episodes being merely comments. Even today footnotes are printed in smaller type than the text. For the same reason, Berlinghieri represented the figure of St. Francis much larger than all the other figures. Giotto likewise painted his men larger than his sheep. By so doing, he drew the spectator's attention to the men. Men being more significant had to be

larger. Was he right or wrong? No rule can be stated. Giotto,
like all artists, was beyond rules; or better still, like all artists,
he made his own rules. If, by altering the proportions of
nature, Giotto succeeded in realizing what he wanted to do,
he was right; if not, he was wrong. Both proportion and disproportion are but components of the work, and not the
whole of the work. And it is the whole, not the single components, which counts in the artistic result. Giotto's disproportion is only an approach to this goal. It is right if the
goal is reached.

We must follow a similar path in order to understand the
representation of the mountain in Giotto's picture. Gertrude
Stein believes that a poet must say "a rose is a rose." An art
critic must say that in a painting a mountain is not a mountain, but an artistic image. Looking at the *Resurrection* by
Piero della Francesca (fig. 7), or at *The Bridge at Narni*
by Corot (fig. 33), one realizes that mountains for Giotto,
Piero, and Corot are thoroughly different images. In Giotto,
the disproportion between mountain and men is evident.
It is justified by the same reasons already mentioned in
support of the disproportions of his sheep. In addition the
images of mountains in painting may have different functions
with different artists. A mountain for Giotto is not a background; the only background being the sky. Against that
background he painted images of rocks and trees as well as
of men. Mountains for Corot are images of a distant horizon.
A mountain for Giotto is a block of rocks, possessing its own
qualities: depth, heaviness, solidity, hardness, and the breaks
that geologic convulsions have wrought in it. All these qualities have been represented by Giotto very simply, summarily

17

but very effectively, by some light strokes, which emphasize the clear cut of the rocks. A strong sense of reality is inherent in the rocks of Giotto; but it is not the reality of mountains; it is the reality of the above qualities: heaviness, solidity, hardness, etc.

Furthermore, the mountain, with its disproportions, emphasizes the figures of the men not only by contrast, as the sheep do, but actively. The illuminated or half-shaded zones in the mountain are larger than those in the men, and their contrast is sharpened by their clear-cut edges. They emphasize plasticity. Modern critics have very often used the word plasticity and have given it many meanings, thus engendering confusion. Early critics spoke of *relief* when they wanted to indicate the sculptural character of an image in painting. Recently this sculptural character has been called *plastic form,* has been extended from the images to the compositions, and has been considered the essential element in painting. Finally, in order to emphasize the fact that plastic form is a quality in itself, modern critics called this quality "plasticity." In doing so they disregard pictorial form, which is fundamentally different from the plastic one, but which is of value in attaining artistic results. Also these critics pretend to ignore those qualities in painting which are beyond visualization in plastic form, thus confusing a single element, such as plastic form, with the totality of the work of art.

Let us try to define, that is to delimit, the meaning of relief — or plastic form. When one looks at a white marble statue against a gray wall with the light coming from the side, he sees some parts of the figure lighter, and some darker. The lighter parts seem to advance towards the spectator,

18

while the darker parts seem to withdraw in depth. This effect of advancing and withdrawing is what we call *relief*. Form in relief occupies not only two dimensions — height and width — but also the third dimension — depth. Therefore any form in relief produces a three-dimensional effect.

The technique in painting which produces the appearance of relief is called *chiaroscuro,* that is, the contrast or the gradation of light and dark tones, independent of the different colors used in producing them. When the relief of an image is realized through chiaroscuro one may say that the painter has attained a *plastic effect* or a *plastic form*.

Looking at Giotto's painting one sees that the mountain has a remarkable plastic form. It comes forward in the center and goes back at the sides. By advancing at the center it emphasizes the relief of the two young men; by retiring at the left it forms a kind of niche for the figure of the old man.

The figures are draped in very simple garments, with few folds. The contours follow sharp and generally straight lines, widening at the bottom, and expanded inside the figures by the nuance of chiaroscuro. Thus their relief, their occupation of space in depth, and their solidity on the ground are perfectly realized. However, their appearance is not that of statues sculptured in the round, but of high reliefs — high enough to show the depth of their bodies, yet at the same time not so high as to minimize their extension on the surface. The figures have the same solidity as the mountain.

If one looks at the works of Berlinghieri (fig. 4) or of Simone Martini (fig. 5), a younger contemporary of Giotto's, one sees that the figures in their paintings have much less relief, that these artists do not care, as much as Giotto does, for plastic form. Giotto's desire for plastic effect stems from his impulse towards *structure*. The idea of structure becomes clear when one thinks of construction in architecture. A building may reveal its internal construction on its surface. This external appearance is called the *structural effect*. If, on the contrary, the surface shows its own artistic aim, without any concern for the internal construction, its effect is *decorative*. Therefore, in architecture the two effects of structure and decoration are clearly distinguishable. In painting, however, the word *structure* does not have a proper meaning as in architecture, but has instead a metaphorical use to emphasize in a figure the appearance of its internal organization. Berlinghieri and Simone Martini show much less structure than Giotto, because they sought different effects. Giotto concentrated his attention on structure, in which neither his predecessors nor his contemporaries had deep interest. Accordingly we become aware of a new characteristic in Giotto's painting, and this can be found not only in the human figures but also in the rocks of the mountain. In fact, the simplicity of his men and rocks may be explained by the emphasis Giotto places on the structure of things.

Concerning the composition of Giotto's picture, a comparison with Simone Martini's *Annunciation* (fig. 5), is quite instructive. Simone has arranged his two figures of the Archangel Gabriel and the Madonna under three arches, suggesting the division of the surface into three fields: the left arch for Gabriel, the central one for the vase of lilies and the Holy Spirit surrounded by seraphim and descending towards the Madonna, and the right arch for the Madonna. The figures of both Gabriel and the Madonna extend beyond their areas, bringing them closer to each other, but they nevertheless belong to their separate areas, which is emphasized by the wings of the archangel. This clearly shows that the composition adapts the figures to the external architecture of the three arches. This indicates a lack of structure. The architecture of the composition is external. It stems from the arch, instead of from the figures. For this same reason there is a definite lack of depth. It is true that the throne of the Madonna is depicted on a plane receding behind the plane where Gabriel is kneeling. But this is insufficient indication to give depth. Notice that the mantle of the Madonna ends at the foreground. In other words, Simone Martini's composition is on the surface while the composition of Giotto's is in depth.

This seems contradicted by the fact that Giotto's figures of the three men are virtually in the same plane. But here again the mountain helps: low at the left and high at the right, making the general trend of the composition diagonal. And a diagonal line on the surface always brings a suggestion of third dimension. In fact, the high rock at the right seems more distant than the low rock at the left. And in order to counterbalance the composition Giotto painted a high tree at the left and emphasized the relief of the old man. Also the fact that the old man seems to be moving from left to right helps the general direction of the composition, from the foreground towards the middle ground. The sense of depth in each single figure is of course much stronger than in the entire composition. Here is Giotto's evident intention of showing a depth without interfering with the space on the surface, an intention which is clear also in his desire to show apparent reliefs, instead of round statues, as we have already said.

21

To complete the description of the two kinds of composition painted by Simone Martini and by Giotto, it is well to meditate on the meaning of two words often used in art criticism: *pattern* and *design*. Pattern is the decorative design as executed on carpet, wallpaper, etc. Its meaning connotes the idea of a model from which a thing is to be made. Design means plan, purpose, or a preliminary sketch of a picture. The difference consists, therefore, in the greater freedom attributed to the idea of design, where the accent is on invention, on purpose; while the idea of pattern stresses the application, or the execution of a model, as in carpets.

Of course, Simone Martini invented his own composition; but by so doing he bowed to convention—he accepted a traditional three-arched form for the surface, which he emphasized by a repeated rhythm of undulating lines. One can say, therefore, that Simone created his design from a pre-established pattern. On the other hand, we find no pattern at all in Giotto's picture. And in spite of the "finished" quality of his work, the design appears as though it had been created extemporaneously following an intimate necessity of structural plasticity and ignoring any other ideal of vision. His work, therefore, is an exceptional example of pure design.

We may also approach Giotto's vision from another angle —by observing the static character of his figures. Of course this does not mean that his figures are immobile or rigid, like the *St. Francis* of Berlinghieri (fig. 4). The structural solidity of Giotto's figures suggests a character which seems motionless, but which is actually not static. Movement in painting is of course metaphorical, but no doubt, as we shall see later, the suggestion of very lively movement has often been realized by some painters. For Giotto's work it is enough to say that the static character of his figures emphasizes a restrained energy which finds expression in potential movement.

In spite of a certain lack of energy, a much greater movement may be noted in Simone Martini (fig. 5). His undulating lines suggest a continuous movement, like the running of placid waves. However, this is not merely an artificial or abstract movement, because it emphasizes the movement of Gabriel towards the Madonna and her shy withdrawal from him. It goes beyond the mere representation of the figures by deliberately stressing the moving lines.

Also in order to understand the use Giotto makes of *color*, a comparison with Simone's painting is very useful. Here, in this connection, I'd like to remind the reader of the three schematic properties of color — quality, intensity and tonality. The following diagram represents a schematic wheel of color-properties:

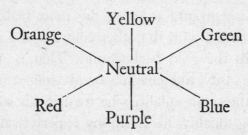

The *neutral* includes all the gradations of gray, from white to black, which are in painting no colors at all. Yellow, green, blue, purple, red and orange are called *qualities* of color. The qualities which are represented on the wheel as opposite to each other, for example red and green, are called *complementaries*.

23

The *intensity* of each quality depends on its distance from the neutral. The *tonality* is the effect of light and shade suggested by color. This effect can be realized in two ways. By *chiaroscuro,* that is, by the nearness of two neutrals to each other, one whiter and the other blacker. This effect is not, of course, tonality, in the real sense of the word, because it is not made by colors, but by neutrals. The *effect of light and shade* becomes a tonality when it is realized by the qualities of colors, one functioning as light, the other as shadow. An extremely brilliant yellow placed near a less brilliant purple is a typical example of a schematic tonality. To distinguish this style of effect from chiaroscuro we shall call it *light and shade.* The difference is one of conception rather than of execution. Chiaroscuro is an effect of light and shade realized through neutrals, and seen as neutrals; light and shade is an effect realized through colors seen as qualities.

If we apply these color schemes to Simone Martini's painting, we can readily understand his color harmony. In the original the background is gold, the most brilliant yellow one finds in nature, with the other colors of the images harmonizing with the gold background. That is, they are of the utmost intensity, like enamels or precious stones. Within the limits of the single qualities he used in his coloring, and while ignoring tonality, his harmony is perfect and enchanting. The gradation of the shadows in the faces, the hands, and in some of the folds of his figures was necessary to diminish the intensity of the qualities of his color scheme. But this sporadic lessening of intensity has no influence on the color harmony as a whole.

Giotto's picture is a fresco; a fresco is painted on a wall,

24

where a gold background is never used. Thus Giotto painted a background of blue sky, quite a dark blue. Black would have been too sharp, too mournful, for Giotto's vital imagination. But the blue he used has the function of black in relation to the other colors, which are white green for the rocks, and white rose for the draperies. The general effect of his color harmony is thus an almost white against an almost black, a real effect of chiaroscuro, with the colors giving it their vibrating vitality without essentially modifying it. The contrast between the color system of Simone and that of Giotto could not possibly be greater. Simone realizes his desire for perfection in externalizing his extreme preciousness, while Giotto realizes his perfection by rendering the structure of his fresco more and more intimate at the expense of its external appearance.

Giotto is considered the founder of Western realism. What we have said concerning the proportions which he employed to represent human figures and natural objects in his painting seems to contradict this opinion. Realism is a word of too many meanings, and for an understanding of Giotto it is better to stick to the idea of concreteness in contradistinction to abstraction. Many abstract components exist in the works of Giotto — the lines of his draperies, the surfaces of his rocks, hierarchical proportions, etc. But since all terms in art criticism are relative, a comparison between the *Head of Christ* by Giotto (fig. 2) and the other *Head of Christ* by an Anonymous Master of the thirteenth century (fig. 3) shows the concreteness of Giotto and the abstractness of the Anonymous Master. Here, again, I want to emphasize that "concrete" and "abstract" have no absolute values. Even though the *Christ* of Giotto is an exalting masterpiece, the *Christ* of the Anonymous Master, too, has a perfection of its own. The latter's rendering of the Christ is abstract, the simplified suggestion of a human head notwithstanding, because the lines forming the head do not stem from any experience of the human form. The aim of the painter was to express his conception of the Christ through abstract lines and sharp contrasts of light and dark colors. The lines and color contrasts are violent in order to express in themselves a violent mood; their power is therefore greater because they are abstract.

Concreteness always denotes a gradation of forms and colors, as well as of emotions. Some of the lines setting off the head of Christ by Giotto are sharp, as for example those forming the nose and the eyes, but the chiaroscuro employed in modeling the cheeks, the forehead, the hair, and through these, the face, is full of gradations which suggest its structure. As the beard is loose, this creates an effect which is entirely pictorial. Therefore the artistic effect of the whole is more one of nuance than one of abstract simplification, but no less powerful, because Giotto's power is one derived from deep human experience, which is lacking in the Anonymous Master's work. In comparison with Giotto, the Anonymous Master's form shows something of a scheme which is an abstraction—a scheme, an accent without a word, a symbol. And a symbol can be extremely powerful, but is never representative.

Every artist worthy of the name puts a soul in the body he paints. The usual way of suggesting a soul is to tell a story. The story told in figure 1 by Giotto is the following: Joachim had been married to Annah for twenty years without having had any children, and for this reason a priest expelled him from the temple. Ashamed, Joachim did not go back home, but withdrew to his shepherds in the country. Later on, Joachim was told to go back home, where a daughter was to be born: she was Mary, Mother of God. Giotto chose for his scene the meeting of Joachim with his shepherds. Joachim, grieved by his expulsion from the temple, is sad; his head is bowed and his hands clasp his mantle close about him. He wants to be alone. The small dog recognizes him and comes to comfort him. The two shepherds understand that something is wrong with Joachim. They stop and look at each other questioningly. That is the story. It is clear and bare, like the rocks.

To understand better the real character of the feeling expressed by Giotto through his story it would be helpful to compare his *Head of Christ* (fig. 2) with the *Head of Christ* by the Anonymous thirteenth-century Master (fig. 3) and with Berlinghieri's *St. Francis* (fig. 4). Figure 3 reveals the precise intention of awakening pity in the spectator. The reduction of Christ to a symbol of cruel suffering is powerfully realized, since the more abstract the form, the more violent is the emotion expressed. Similarly, figure 4 shows a very abstract figure with the forms of the open hand, the ears, and the beard accenting the abstraction. And the very rigidity of the whole figure also denotes an abstraction. But Berlinghieri's purpose is to arouse a very different emotion. The sacred image dominates the whole picture. The six episodes of the Saint's life — depicted on each side of the Saint — in their smallness, variety, and movement also exalt the very rigidity and immensity of the sacred image. What Berlinghieri sought to do by this sacred image was to arouse in the spectator a feeling of reverence and adoration. Saint Francis was the saint who spoke to the birds, and the panels illustrate the story of the birds listening to him. St. Francis died in 1226, only nine years before this picture was painted. But nothing of the Saint, as he was on earth, remains in this sacred image. The fact of his being St. Francis had no importance for the artist. What was important to him was the symbolic image to be adored, and to enhance this adoration he painted the Saint to look like an apparition — an apparition which does not belong to mankind, but to Heaven, among angels and seraphim. The artist, no doubt, thought that the more unearthly and transcendental his image of the Saint, the stronger and the more effective would be the appeal to adoration.

Giotto was more concrete in his *Head of Christ*. His divinity is more deeply rooted in the human heart. Therefore Giotto's *Christ* has an emotional appeal less violent than that of the *Christ* by the Anonymous thirteenth-century Master, and less absolute than that of the *St. Francis* by Berlinghieri, but it is nevertheless much more complex and convincing. The pity aroused for the thirteenth-century *Christ* is absolute, but human emotion is relative: the absolute in emotion lacks nuances, discrimination and humanity. This pity is determined by cruelty, but both cruelty and pity, in spite of their strength, are not individualized here. They are abstract symbols of cruelty and pity. In other words, the feeling aroused by the suffering of this *Christ* is abstract, as is its drawing.

The same must be said of Berlinghieri's *St. Francis*. The

28

feeling of adoration aroused by the image of the Saint is due entirely to the abstract idea of the sacred image and not to the individuality of the Saint as a sacred person. This image is different from all other contemporary images because it approaches the abstract idea of an image more closely than the others. Hence its power and its abstract feeling—as abstract, in fact, as its drawing.

Giotto does not inspire pity for a victim of cruelty nor adoration for a sacred image. He suggests sympathy, devotion and love. His Christ is suffering, but His suffering is more moral than physical. It is human and dignified. In His sadness there is forgiveness. His expression shows how conscious He is of His executioners' wrongdoing, while His open mouth portrays the suffering of human pain. This fusion of divine and human feeling—where the divine embracing the human represents the moral victory of man—is the greatness of Giotto's Christ.

Now we can better understand the source of the dignity of Joachim and his good-hearted shepherds. The source is Giotto's consciousness of the divine in the nature of man.

Simone Martini (*c.* 1284–1344) was a younger contemporary of Giotto. He came from Siena, and Giotto from Florence. The two towns are only a few miles apart, but their history followed a different course, so that Simone and Giotto really lived in two different worlds. The scene of Simone Martini (fig. 5) represents the *Annunciation,* the moment when the Archangel Gabriel announces to Mary that she will soon become the Mother of God. Simone's conception of an angel is that of a very fine-looking young man—tall and slender, slightly effeminate, profusely ornamented and

crowned with a laurel wreath, like a poet. He has just de-
scended from Heaven, with his wings still poised for flight
and his mantle still flapping in the air. His sudden arrival
would no doubt have disconcerted the Madonna. But the
archangel, with grace and charm and supreme elegance, re-
assures the Madonna by his act of kneeling in feigned humility. The Madonna is a little frightened by his appearance,
but since she too is a highly refined personage she knows how
to transform her shock into a well composed movement with
supreme charm and elegance. This accent on elegance and
charm is more worldly than heavenly. It belongs to a very
exclusive world, a very refined life at court.

If Giotto expressed his feeling of the divine in the common
man, he knew that the common man represented the whole
of humanity. The divine is a creation of man, of man as
man in general, not just of a special class of men. Christ
understood this, and so did Giotto. But, on the contrary,
Simone Martini saw the divine in the mere exclusiveness of
a class, in the character of an aristocracy, and by emphasizing
that class he lost sight of humanity as well as of divinity.

So far, this analysis has dealt with what we have seen in
the various paintings considered, that is, with the components
of the individual pictures. We saw how line, plastic form,
color, composition, statics and movement, abstraction, concreteness and the expression of emotion, were conceived by
different painters. And we have also tried to grasp some hint
of the general attitude of each painter towards his work. But
this attitude has appeared to us only fragmentarily. Now
we must try to understand whether this attitude is constant,

and whether it moulds each separate component of a painting, and all of them together, in the same way.

In his paintings Giotto (*c.* 1266–1337) subordinates the
natural proportions of things to suit both his ideal of a
divinized man and the plastic solidity of his images. His line
as well as his chiaroscuro is made to serve this solidity, while
his color is adapted to the expression of this plastic solidity.
Thus each thing represented, a man as well as a mountain,
is visualized as a thing in itself, rather than as a relationship
of things. But a relationship exists, not of things, but of plastic
effects, a plastic accord among images each standing by itself.
To emphasize the isolation of his images, Giotto accentuates
their contours, and to preserve their accord he stresses the
homogeneity of their plastic forms. Thus he fully achieves
a balance between isolation and accord. The purpose of this
is to balance the structure of each image with the whole, and
to demonstrate the functional relationship between the plastic
bodies on the surface and their occupation of space in depth.
Therefore Giotto shuns all surface pattern, and instead creates a design that includes both surface and depth. This is
an act of freedom versus tradition. However, this act of
creation implies no strain in his work, but springs naturally
from the intimate necessity of concentrating his creative
power on plastic structural effects. This concentration is responsible for his exclusions. He excludes movement. His
bodies being severely self-contained must remain static, but
for this very reason their interior lines and modeling give
them a greater energy. Therefore the more static they appear
the more by contrast they suggest energy and potential movement — which is life.

In their plastic quality his colors, too, reveal a touch of life in spite of their being subordinated to chiaroscuro. All this is abstract as well as realistic: it is abstract because plasticity, which in itself is an abstraction, conditions the images; and it is realistic because the structure of things emphasizes their concreteness. The relationship between the abstractness and concreteness of his bodies corresponds to the relation between the divine and the human in the souls he represents in his paintings. When the divine becomes human the result is sympathy and love; when the human becomes divine the result is moral greatness and dignity. And for this reason Giotto allows no movement and ornament in his bodies, and he also allows no distinction of class or culture in the souls he creates. His man is the common man; and therefore he is man in his universal aspect.

All these components of Giotto's painting are but the expression of the artist's personality. Who is this artist who dared divorce himself from the tradition of abstract form and transcendental content, which constituted the tradition before him? The legend concerning his origin and his talent agree on one point: Giotto was a man of the people and had the soundness and directness of the people. He understood St. Francis's message of humility and love, and most of his work was dedicated to the Saint's churches. But Giotto's temperament was quite different from that of the Saint; he was deeply rooted in the earth. His love was concrete, and he expressed this concreteness in the consistency with which he painted the human figure and nature. In his love there was something of the same popular daring with which the people exalted the life of the Communes in Italy, and especially in Florence, where through their struggles and troubles a free self-government developed and flourished. In Giotto's time the dawn of a new civilization appeared, which was later to become known as the Renaissance.

This civilization was based on man's impulse towards freedom, breaking away from all transcendental sanction to faith in man's values. In painting, Giotto discovered that this new faith in man had to be expressed through structure, plasticity, and simplicity. And he discovered it without effort, so that his approach to this new form of faith was direct, immediate, and naïve. Plastic and structural qualities, as well as the transmutation of the divine into the human, can be found in some later artists. But none of them was more direct, immediate, and naïve in his attitude than was Giotto, towards his images, which consisted of a saint, some shepherds, and a mountain. And it is this attitude which gives the tone to all his other qualities, and explains them. He could not indulge in movement, ornaments, refinements, details. He wanted certainty, which in painting means solidity, intimacy, structure, moral values, and countenance. And he stuck to the essentials, which he discovered in the structure of the bodies and the humanity of the souls he painted. Therefore he knew how to reunite Heaven and earth.

Both his predecessors, Berlinghieri and the Anonymous Master of the *Head of Christ,* stuck to abstraction and transcendency. Their devotion was born of respect and adoration, rather than of love. Their individual expression was powerful and perfect, but narrow. They did not see the divine in man, and therefore they created symbols, either of suffering and piety, or of adoration. Their creations were, in a sense, the

33

revelation of a law rather than the revelation of human life.

Simone Martini, on the other hand, still followed certain traditional forms which he found appropriate to his imagination. He cared for all the qualities Giotto excluded: movement, ornaments, refinement, details. He longed for a value Giotto ignored: beauty. Giotto was too spiritual to care for physical beauty, and too human to care for celestial beauty. But Simone Martini wanted celestial beauty. And he found a subtle, delicate grace—a flower. But a flower grown in a greenhouse. He mistook the worldly life of a court for the divine life, and mundane beauty for celestial beauty. He sought the distinction, refinement, and exclusiveness of the aristocracy. Therefore he lost something both of the divine and the human. His personality was narrower than that of Giotto. But within his limitations, he too found his perfection, a very gentle and sweet one. France had invented the poetry of the courts of love. Simone Martini became the greatest painter of the courts of love.

Chapter Two

Fig. 6. MASACCIO: *Expulsion of Adam and Eve from Paradise,* c. 1425.

Fig. 7. PIERO DELLA FRANCESCA: *Resurrection*, c. 1460.

Fig. 8. ANTONIO POLLAIUOLO: *Rape of Dejanira, c.* 1467.

Fig. 9. SANDRO BOTTICELLI: *Spring*, c. 1475.

Fig. 10. LEONARDO DA VINCI: *The Virgin of the Grotto*, 1483–90.

Chapter Two

THE DISCOVERY OF MAN

THE FIVE illustrations reproduced in this chapter provide a general idea of the main trends of painting in Florence during the fifteenth century. They have influenced the whole course of art in later centuries and especially in modern times.

If Giotto is the great forerunner of modern art, Masaccio is its founder. Masaccio's painting, the *Expulsion of Adam and Eve from Paradise* (fig. 6), represents a man and a woman coming out of a door. From the sky an angel orders them to go. In the background are some hills, now blurred by the ravages of time, and the sky. The attention of the artist is concentrated on Adam and Eve. The rest is only accompaniment. The door is high enough for the people to pass through, but its presence in the picture is only symbolical. Its proportions are theoretically possible but not actually convincing. That is, its symbolic character, like that of Giotto's mountain, remains even if the proportions be corrected. The same thing applies to the angel: that is, his presence in the picture, his proportion and his position in three-dimensional space, are justified by his act of expulsion rather than by the fact that he is flying. Finally, the landscape functions merely as a background, as does the sky: a hill is for Masaccio not an image in itself, as it is for Giotto, but a suggestion of space in which to place his figures. Thus, in Masaccio, too, we find an order of importance in his elements: door, angel, and landscape are subordinated to the figures of Adam and Eve.

Giotto's figures as well as his rocks show the same plastic character. Whereas the plastic character of Masaccio, being concentrated on the human figures, emphasizes the unity of the effect. The consequence of this is that the plastic form of Masaccio's figures is stronger than that of Giotto's. If a Giotto figure suggests a relief, Masaccio's figures suggest a statue in the round. These two different effects are realized by a different treatment of the chiaroscuro. The contour lines which in Giotto's pictures are still sharp, in Masaccio's are much softer. In the *Expulsion of Adam and Eve from Paradise* the light comes from the right, so that the parts of the figures towards the right are illuminated while those towards the left are in shadow. There is a plastic continuity of the contours towards the inner surfaces, and a precise demarcation of the most relieved points where the light ends and the shade begins. If in Giotto's work there is a succession of clear and dark tones, in Masaccio's there is a unique transition from light to shade; and thus the plastic solidity of his figures is thereby immensely strengthened. The naïve early critics who were astonished by Masaccio's plastic power said that he was the first painter who knew how to represent

figures firmly planted on the ground. In comparison with
Giotto's plasticity, it is obvious that such an impression is
justified by Masaccio's ability in rendering the mass and
weight of his figures.

Masaccio emphasizes the coherent structure of his figures
to such an extent that any pattern disappears, sacrificed to
the structure. The composition is diagonal; Adam and Eve,
as well as the door and the angel, are conceived in depth.
And this realization of depth is so pronounced that Giotto's
diagonal composition appears, in comparison, only symbolical. The space left empty in the picture is very limited, and
the contrast between the narrow space and the big mass of
the figures is very pronounced; a contrast which places a
new emphasis on the figures. They assume a monumental
value. The sense of humility characteristic of the figures of
Giotto has disappeared. A new faith in human beings em-
powers Masaccio to see man greater than he appears to be,
more energetic, more resolute, more heroic — man assuming
the proportions of monuments. No ornament can be added
to such a grandeur. Any ornament would detract from that
severe unity which gives it the effect of monumentality.

Also, the check which Giotto has placed on movement is
now released. Masaccio's movement is not only potential; it
is real, even if it is restrained. It is a movement at once limited and emphasized by the weight of the figures. Its reality
is accompanied by a greater potentiality, which makes it
more self-evident and convincing.

Concerning Masaccio's coloring we know very little, but
one thing can be said: that he stressed chiaroscuro, and therefore the graduation of neutrals, extending the shadowy parts

37

in order to emphasize relief. Sometimes, however, he gives some hints of going beyond chiaroscuro and suggesting light and shade through the qualities of color. But this rarely happens in his painting. When it does, it is the exception rather than the rule, since his main coloring was based on chiaroscuro.

As for realism, it is evident that Masaccio's ability to impress us with his sense of reality is much greater than Giotto's. This is the result of his round figures, with their weight, unity, and movement. However, we find there are some distortions in Masaccio which are even more daring than Giotto's, and exaggeration of form always means the substitution of symbolic motives for the real ones. Eve's face is distorted by her despair. Adam drags his right leg along in an unnatural way in order to show the symbolic effort made in leaving the door. And we have seen in the thirteenth-century Master's *Christ* (fig. 3) how symbolic abstractions can heighten the expression of what the artist wants to express. But Masaccio's abstractions of natural forms have a thoroughly different character. The abstractions of figure 3 do not derive from a knowledge of nature but from a tradition of abstract design. Masaccio's abstractions, on the other hand, presuppose a knowledge of nature, and are the result of a rebellion against natural limitations in order to attain a more powerful expression. The thirteenth-century Master's abstractions belong to an order outside of nature; those of Masaccio belong to the order of nature. They create a new nature, the nature of painting, with full consciousness of the nature of things. At the risk of seeming paradoxical, we must stress that this was Masaccio's power: he was concrete even in his abstractions. This fondness for the concrete is, in Masaccio, unparalleled. A look at figures 7, 8, 9 and 10 will show that neither Piero della Francesca, Pollaiuolo, Botticelli, nor Leonardo da Vinci was as concrete as Masaccio.

Masaccio's concreteness, however, has nothing to do with materialism. His story is clearly expressed. The angel orders Adam and Eve to go. His power is symbolized by the sword, and his authority is evident in the gesture of his left arm. Yet this is still accompaniment. The principal theme of the story is the depiction of Adam and Eve's expulsion from paradise. Adam is ashamed, turns upon himself, and covers his face with his hands. Eve is openly desperate and cries. Masaccio's psychological insight is very penetrating: the different reactions of a man and a woman before a moral disaster, such as expulsion from paradise, embodies the character of eternal humanity and is thoroughly convincing.

However, it must be made clear here that Masaccio's sympathy for what happened to Adam and Eve has nothing to do with the appreciation of his art. We have already said that those who fall in love with the hero of a novel, cannot understand the art of the writer. Similarly, but conversely, those who believe that Masaccio's art consists only, or even mainly, in his plastic form, will not be able to understand how his plastic forms are prompted by an inner compulsion.

In order to understand Masaccio's attitude towards his figures, in a physical and in a moral sense, it is well to remember that Masaccio died at the age of twenty-seven in 1429. Yet in spite of his brief span of life he was the founder of Renaissance painting; that is, he became imbued with the spirit of the times, the spirit of a new humanistic civilization which drew its strength from a new knowledge of man. He represented his plastic form through a new synthesis; he discovered a new relationship between man and space according to a new perspective, he emphasized the weight of the body, and knew how to give this weight movement, convincing every one who saw his paintings of the concreteness of his creations as well as of their monumentality. Conscious of the nuances of chiaroscuro as well as of human behavior, he realized the drama between a superhuman order of things and human despair, stressing the moral endeavor of mankind to reconcile the two orders of things, the divine and the human, nor was he afraid to distort natural forms in order better to emphasize his expression of them.

Humanism was concerned with moral problems, and aimed at a reform of the religious tradition without departing from the attitude of the Middle Ages towards Christianity. From St. Francis of Assisi, or from the thirteenth century onward, Italians took very little interest in theological problems. They dreamed of a happy brotherhood of men, and loved all things on earth, with a new intensity of feeling that projected Christ and his deeds into the every-day life of man. And at the beginning of the fifteenth century this trend brought about a new faith in man. Every one exalted man as the center of the universe, and deified him. More than any one else in his time, and perhaps even later, Masaccio gave perfect expression to a moral determination to uphold the assurance inspired by the Christian faith. His religion no longer transcends man, it is immanent in man. Yet it still shows the same undiminished strength of religious feeling. Imbued with this faith, Masaccio has no eye for ornament, for details, or for skilful analysis. This concentration results in a formal synthesis, which creates heroes. But in spite of all his concreteness, he is not a realist, because his faith pervaded all reality. And his humanity becomes a legend about moral heroes. He is no longer naïve and humble, as Giotto is: he knows, but his faith overwhelms his knowledge.

This is Masaccio's attitude, impressing his bodies as it does with his human ideal, and establishing the relationship between his sense of plasticity and his knowledge of man. This is the artistic value of Masaccio's work.

Figure 7 reproduces the *Resurrection* by Piero della Francesca. Christ emerges from His tomb with the triumphal banner of the Cross, while four soldiers are still asleep before the tomb. Behind the tomb and Christ, in the middle distance, there is a hilly landscape and, beyond that, the sky.

The first thing one remarks in this painting is the shape and color of the group of figures. The group in the foreground seems as though it were not a part of the landscape, which, by its form and the position of the trees, suggests space in depth, so that the luminous sky appears very distant. But the group does not occupy much space in depth; for in spite of its plastic masses and the foreshortening of the soldiers, it tends to emphasize the composition on the surface. If compared with the *Expulsion of Adam and Eve from Paradise* by Masaccio, Piero della Francesca's group seems a presentation of figures more than a representation of an event. The space which the figures can occupy is much deeper than that used by Masaccio, but Piero della Francesca uses it only as a background for the group of figures in the foreground. The group is shaped like a pyramid, the apex being the head of Christ, and the base, the soldiers. That is, the composition shows a desire for a geometrical form. Christ is a sacred image, fixed for eternity, and shows no movement in emerging from His tomb. The soldiers, too, are immobile, for a reason which is obviously more important than showing that they are asleep — they are crystallized because their shape is formed by regular facets of light. Foreshortening in painting is generally used to express movement, but this is not the case in the work of Piero della Francesca, who prefers immobility. Their pattern is that of the spokes of a wheel, but a wheel immobile for eternity. This immobility is an ideal which transcends concreteness. The soldier seen in profile at the left of the picture shows that the contours of his back and helmet are nothing but geometrical curves, while the facial features of the second soldier from the left emphasize their affinity with geometrical forms. And the tree at the left recalls the form of a column. There is, therefore, in this picture, the *Resurrection,* a conscious trend towards a geometrical order, towards an abstract form. And so it is possible to understand the reason for their immobility, for the grouping of the figures towards a surface. Piero della Francesca does not wish to represent an event, even less a drama or psychological expression. What he wishes is to present forms suggesting a geometrical regularity. Indeed, he even wrote a theory on the regularity of forms.

This striving for a regularity of forms is connected with the discovery of the rules of perspective for painters, made by the architect Brunelleschi, at the beginning of the fifteenth century. We have seen how Giotto treated space in depth. But his sense of space was based on his own instinct or sensibility. When geometrical perspective was discovered, sensibility or instinct gave way to learning and the rules of science. But the Florentine of the fifteenth century was too much the artist to be contented with the mere application of scientific rules. He was enthusiastic about geometry, he felt geometry as an ideal of beauty, and made of perspective an ideal in itself. So, even mathematical abstractions were used to heighten the sensibility of the artist. Piero della Francesca went farther than any other artist of his day; and in his own way he managed to impart an almost divine value to his perspective and his regular forms. He carried out this ideal for regular forms and this feeling for perspective, both in human and natural things. And in spite of the fact that space belongs to the order of nature, it was transformed by Piero della Francesca's perspective into a transcendental frame for his human figures.

This transcendental aim in rendering regular forms, is, however, realized through a pronounced concreteness, attained through both chiaroscuro and colors. Even in a black-and-white reproduction it is easy to see that the relation between light and dark colors is much more complex than in Masaccio's. The figures of Masaccio are as a whole clear against a dark background. In Piero della Francesca's work, on the other hand, the soldiers are dark, and the Christ is luminous; a contrast which is repeated in the dark landscape and luminous sky of the background. The purpose of this rhythm is symbolic: to show that both Christ and sky are flooded with light, while men and earth are left in darkness. But this symbolism becomes concrete through the contrast of the pictorial effect achieved by dark tones against light ones, and of the plastic effect achieved by the light figure of Christ against the dark landscape. This double effect gives the figure of Christ a great power of detachment and evidence.

The fact is that Masaccio's chiaroscuro appears simple and uniform, whereas Piero della Francesca's clear colors represent light against dark colors representing shadow; thus his chiaroscuro is transformed into an effect of light and shade. Masaccio's full-rounded relief is transformed by Piero della Francesca into expansive surfaces, detaching rather than relieving objects. The rhythm of this contrast of light and dark zones can be followed in the details, in the soldiers, as well as in the landscape: this kind of treatment of light and shade results in concreteness. But light, by its very nature, always vibrates. And in Piero della Francesca nothing vibrates; all is immobile. Both the strength of plasticity and the concreteness of light and shade are conditioned by the immobility of geometric forms. For this same reason, the structure of the bodies is very strong; but also a pattern appears, an abstract pattern on the surface.

A similar contrast exists between his realism and idealism. We saw that Masaccio's ideal was rooted in the reality of the event. Piero della Francesca's ideal goes beyond reality. To avoid seeing the radiance of the resurrecting Christ one soldier covers his eyes, while the other three, who are still asleep, suffer from the excessiveness of the radiance. It is this light, not the event, which justifies their relevance in the composition. And the Christ, as we have said, is a luminous, powerful image, an image of contemplation, showing no movement in the act of resurrection. This lack of movement is the source of the symbolic character of Piero della Francesca's figures. He emphasizes his statements to the utmost, but he conceals his emotions behind a longing for contemplation. This is indeed a unique kind of concrete symbolism.

The whole group is monumental, but of a monumentality very different from that of Masaccio. It depends on the geometric pattern rather than on structural synthesis.

Piero della Francesca was born between 1410 and 1420 and died in 1492. He learned the values of plastic form from Masaccio, while from other painters of his day he learned how to make use of colored light and shade and the treatment of space in perspective, but it was by himself that he developed the ideal of symmetrical bodies, geometrical beauty, and the contemplation of immobility. He embraced the humanistic ideal which believed that the divine is immanent in man, in the dignity of man, and that man is the center of the universe. But he interpreted this ideal in an original way. He did not seek the expression of power and energy. He did dream, however, of a dignified serenity, and of a solemnity with charm. This meant a symbolic representation of images, which he succeeded in rendering with such a concreteness, complexity of colors, and light and shade, that he fully realized a balance between the abstract and the concrete. Therefore, it is difficult to say which was greater in him, whether his power of realization or his impulse toward abstraction. In logic a contradiction must be resolved by a synthesis. But in art a contradiction may survive in a balance where contrasting elements exalt each other. And this balance is the very essence of Piero della Francesca's art, the result of his genius.

45

Masaccio enhanced the realization of the human figure in art. Piero della Francesca both developed this realization and blocked it. He enhanced it by his perspective and light, and blocked it by the immobility of his figures and his desire for contemplation.

Antonio Pollaiuolo's *Rape of Dejanira* (fig. 8) shows a new trend, a new emphasis on anatomy and movement. What we see in this picture is a wide landscape in depth, with a far distant horizon. In the foreground there are three figures: at the right is Hercules shooting an arrow across a stream to the Centaur Nessus, who is holding the captive Dejanira. The proportion between figures and landscape is thoroughly different from that of Masaccio or Piero della Francesca. Pollaiuolo does not use the landscape as a mere background. But rather he aims at the pictorial value of the landscape, independently of his figures, which are no longer the center of the composition, subordinated to the function and importance of the landscape.

The treatment of the figures is new, and is based on anatomy and movement. Here a comparison with Masaccio is instructive. Masaccio sees his nudes as moving masses; he does not analyze movement; his movement is an impulse given to a plastic form. The accent of movement is not placed on the contours but on the plastic bodies as wholes. Pollaiuolo, instead, sees movement in a different, even contrary way. His contour is much more delineated than Masaccio's, and it is the succession of the straight and curving lines of the contour which suggests movement. This suggestion of movement is not limited to the contours, but continues inside the bodies with other lines which have the function both of confirming the movement of the contours and of representing the anatomy of the nude. In the figure of Hercules we have a perfect example of how Pollaiuolo combined his search for anatomy with his realizing energy, creative of movement. If we now compare the movement of Pollaiuolo with that of Masaccio, we shall readily understand that the latter achieved movement in his painting through a creative synthesis of impulse and plastic form, whereas Pollaiuolo subjected his interpretation of movement to an anatomical analysis before recomposing his expression in a synthesis.

Pollaiuolo was the most successful Florentine master to profit from the knowledge of anatomy and to draw from it its energizing power. Thus, the figure of Hercules is in itself a masterpiece of its kind.

In the figure of the Centaur Nessus there is even something more. To its movement and anatomy, Pollaiuolo added a pictorial effect of dark surfaces. But in painting Dejanira Pollaiuolo did not dare expose her muscles, which would have destroyed her feminine beauty. He went so far as to stress some abstract geometric elements (the oval of the face, the cylinder of the arm), but without being aware that these geometric forms are obstacles to any movement. This is the reason why the movement of Hercules and the Centaur appears much more natural than that of Dejanira.

However, Pollaiuolo in his search for energy and movement did not limit himself to the use of lines and anatomy. The river which Nessus is crossing is moving rapidly, and its water is foaming. This movement cannot be rendered by lines, but only by touches of light shining through a mass of shadows. The same thing may be said of his landscape, where

47

the succession of dark and light tones gives a certain vibration, and therefore energy and movement.

By comparing Pollaiuolo's treatment of landscape with that of Piero della Francesca (fig. 7), one sees that the latter's is absolutely static, while the former's is energetic and full of movement. In painting there are two kinds of movements, following two different methods of representation. An artist may find the reason for his movement in the interior structure of a figure: in this case the movement is a function of action, and the line is the best means for rendering this kind of expression. Or another artist may see movement outside a figure, enveloping it through a contrast of light and shade: in this case the movement does not result in action, but in a cosmic vibration which impresses with life even a lying or seated figure, and color is the best means for rendering this kind of expression. The first kind of expression stems from the Florentine tradition of plasticity; the second kind of expression goes beyond that tradition and creates pictorial effects. Sporadically, Pollaiuolo uses both kinds.

The dignity of man, the centering of the whole of nature in man, such as we have seen in Masaccio and Piero della Francesca, becomes uncertain in Pollaiuolo's art. Pollaiuolo sees man in action, and he is not interested in depicting man's grandeur, dignity or beauty. He is only interested in depicting man's struggle in life, forcing the whole of nature to participate in his struggle. The nexus between nature and man is closer in Pallaiuolo's art than in any of the previous Florentine artists, and this nexus is movement, that is, a quality which belongs to both nature and man. The order of importance as between man and nature is changed. The center of Pollaiuolo's picture is no longer man but the river, and the drama of the three figures becomes episodic, in spite of their occupying the foreground. We can hardly say that Pollaiuolo wanted to include his figures in the landscape; what he did do was to juxtapose figures and landscape, but the unity of that juxtaposition consists in the quality of movement, pertaining to both nature and man. It was this quality that Pollaiuolo represented, and not the story of Hercules and Dejanira. In fact, Hercules is shown in the stance used in shooting an arrow, rather than in the act itself, while Dejanira is seen showing her despair instead of actually trying to escape. In this translation of action into energy — in this transformation of actuality into potentiality — lies the greatness of Pollaiuolo's art. It is his poetry. None of the fifteenth-century Florentine painters were as fond of action as Pollaiuolo, but the great plastic tradition of Giotto, Masaccio, and Piero della Francesca helped to canalize Pollaiuolo's art towards this quality of energy instead of towards action.

Antonio Pollaiuolo was born in Florence in 1432, and died in Rome, 1498. He was not only a painter, but a sculptor, a goldsmith, and an engraver. He left the impress of his energy on all his work, and always reached a high level of expression of life. He was not a man of masterpieces; in fact, all his works reveal rather more of his research than of his success. He could not stop searching, nor abandon himself to his natural creativity. He was a man of great effort rather than of accomplishment. But every step of his research was very successful, and he foresaw many of the future possibilities of pictorial form.

Figure 9 represents *Spring* by Botticelli. What we see in it is a series of human figures as reliefs of light forms against a dark background. The darkness of the meadow is relieved by the varied colors of the flowers, while the darkness of the trees is brightened by the light of the sky seen through the treetops. The clearness of the meadow and wood is suggestive of the variety of nature; while the dark zones function as background. This contrast between light figures and dark background is more pronounced than in the work of Masaccio, Piero della Francesca or Pollaiuolo. It means that Botticelli simplifies the plastic effect even more than his predecessors. The plastic quality of his work is not so strong as that of Masaccio, because instead of centering the attention on the bodies as a whole, as Masaccio did, Botticelli emphasized their contour lines. His stressing of contour lines is contrary to the intention of Masaccio and Piero della Francesca, and closer to Pollaiuolo's preference. Yet even here the difference between the line of Botticelli and that of Pollaiuolo is still great. The latter uses his line to emphasize energy and movement and to suggest action. Botticelli's movement does not suggest action, but rhythm. The stance of his figures suggests a slow dance; they induce contemplation but do not suggest drama. The same linear rhythm is continued along the surface of the bodies by chiaroscuro—a chiaroscuro more complex, more nuanced, than that of Masaccio. It corresponds to an ideal, and it does not represent anything but itself. This love of line for itself, and the undulating character of the line, are common to both Botticelli and Simone Martini (fig. 5). But Botticelli's balance between line and plasticity does not exist in Simone Martini, where the line determines a pattern and predominates over all other elements of form. Botticelli's form is a plastic one, and his line is a function of his plasticity. Botticelli has been called the "greatest poet of line." There are many "poets of line," even great ones, but we can readily understand this enthusiasm for Botticelli's line, because it is very subtle and delicate, and because one cannot specify where the line ends and the plasticity begins. This very moment of transmutation is the real source of Botticelli's grace.

In the individual compositions of both Masaccio and Pollaiuolo structure predominates over pattern. In Botticelli, on the contrary, the pattern is again emphasized. The third dimension is renounced: what Botticelli sought is to reveal figures on the surface, at once deep but not suggestive of space. Masaccio reveals the despair of Adam and Eve; Pollaiuolo reveals the fury of Hercules, but Botticelli does not reveal any overpowering emotion at all. He lyrically expresses his own mood, his desire for grace. For subject matter, he substitutes a motif which is itself identified with his lines and chiaroscuro.

However, to understand Botticelli's picture as a whole it is necessary to analyze his subject matter. The first image at the left represents Mercury; then come the Three Graces; standing quite apart and farther back of them is Venus; above her, however, is Cupid with his inevitable bow and arrow; then, you see Flora garbed in flowers; next to her is a young woman, very lightly veiled, representing Spring itself. She is being ushered in by the figure of a young man representing Zephyr, the wind. In order to understand how Botticelli could think of painting this series of figures, unrelated to one another, in any single action, we must first study his literary sources. It was Lucretius, the Latin poet, in his *De Rerum Natura,* who first linked the idea of Venus with the idea of Spring. And later the Florentine poet, Poliziano—who was a friend and contemporary of Botticelli—also wrote about the relation between Venus and Spring. In an ode by the Latin poet Horace, we find mention of the relation of Venus to the Three Graces, and to Mercury. Thus in Latin and contemporary poetry Botticelli found a theme suited to his fancy through which he could portray his beautiful figures. This psychological attitude towards his subject matter was not very different from that of Lucretius, who in his "Invocation to Venus" sang:

> Spring approaches with Venus, preceded by the winged forerunner of the Goddess, while in the path of Zephyr, Flora, his mother, opens the road for them, along which she has strewn an abundance of the most delightful colors and perfumes.

And:

> It is by thee that every living thing should be conceived and should see the sunlight upon emerging from the darkness: before thee, O Goddess, at thy approach, the winds vanish, the clouds disperse; along thy path the industrious earth strews the sweetest flowers, the surface of the sea smiles at thee, and the becalmed sky shines with an overwhelming light. For as soon as the springlike atmosphere of the days returns, and the fruitful breath of Favonius, bursting its bonds, recovers its power, from that very moment, the birds will serenade thee with their melodies, O Goddess.

Even closer in spirit are some verses of Poliziano's *Giostra,* describing the realm of Venus wherein the Graces disport themselves, every beautiful woman's hair is adorned with flowers, and where lascivious Zephyr flies by to catch Flora and in passing causes the meadows to flower.

Botticelli's *Spring* is thus seen to be *poetry in painting,* not only in the sense that every creative painting has a poetic value, but also in the more restricted sense that it illustrates a theme already treated in poetry.

And now let us enquire in what way did the literary sources influence the poetic value of Botticelli's picture? Alberti, a Florentine writer, said that the Graces, holding one another by the hand, are symbols of liberality. Certainly this served as suggestion to Botticelli for his grouping of the Graces. Yet it is evident that the artistic value of the figures does not depend exactly on the fact that they hold one another by the hand, although at the same time one cannot imagine the rhythm of the Graces without this physical contact. Thus, their artistic value does not consist in their plasticity alone, nor in their visual symbolism alone; it goes beyond both.

The same thing can be said of the other poetic motives treated in this picture. Zephyr, a wind, represented by a young man holding the fugitive Flora, the figure of Spring adorned with flowers, the flowering meadow, are all poetic motives that it would also be possible to represent in a form entirely different from that of Botticelli. Botticelli lacked Lucretius's complete faith in nature, nor did he have the almost childish imagination of Poliziano. His love of nature was conditioned by his belief that nature should be subordinated to the idealized human figure, and his sensuous fancy was held in check by his Christian consciousness of the fall of man. Therefore a melancholy sentiment pervades his natural images, transforming the ideal of beauty, full and sound, into

53

an ideal of *grace,* more subtle, more spiritualized and less sound than beauty. This sentiment in Botticelli cannot be defined; any definition is in terms of logic, and sentiment is beyond the confines of logic. Perhaps it can best be suggested by a metaphor. If you think of what Venus meant to the pagan world and to the imagination of Lucretius, you will be aware that Venus was for Botticelli no longer a goddess, but a fallen angel.

The vision of a divine grace pervaded by the melancholy consciousness of its human decay, was the ideal of Botticelli and the very source of his imagination. In different accents it speaks through all his works, both profane and religious, in his Venuses and in his Madonnas. It is this ideal which set Botticelli apart from his contemporaries and made him a solitary artist; and which makes us feel how modern, how near to us, he is with his uncertainty and his repentance. This, in short, is the reason for the tremendous artistic appeal of Botticelli's work.

Now, having considered the form and the subject matter of *Spring,* let us say a few words about its social environment. The picture was painted to decorate a wall in the house of a member of the Medici family, a relative of Lorenzo de' Medici, who was then the master of Florence. Humanism had spread the desire for mythological scenes, whether written or painted. A reconstruction of the realm of Venus, inspired by several poets, was the intention of the picture. It was not an event to be re-enacted, but a pagan world to be contemplated. In this sense *Spring* is a purely decorative painting, like a tapestry. And this also helps us to account for its character of presenting images instead of telling a story.

No doubt the decorative purpose of the composition was con-
genial to Botticelli's artistic talent, because he could thus
concentrate his attention on figures, and let his fancy wander
as it pleased. But the decorative character is only one feature.
What the painting chiefly realizes is the expression of an ideal
of grace, of that special grace belonging to Botticelli which
we have tried to suggest. The social function of the painting
was therefore only a pretext, though a good pretext, for the
achievement of a work of art.

We have discussed Botticelli's line, his plastic form, his
composition of successive figures on a surface, his sense of
beauty and grace, his leaning towards pagan mythology and
Christian legend, his moral restraint, his hesitation between
two worlds, his mood of contemplation, his mode of expression, and his adornment and decoration. Form, color, composition, emotional content, subject matter, social appeal —
all these constitute the components of Botticelli's work. All
can be analyzed by historical knowledge. But the *art* of Botticelli remains, and defies analysis. What, then, does it consist
in? All these components might exist in an inferior painter,
for example one of the numerous Florentine painters of "Cas-
soni," that is, painters of chests or other household furniture.
Therefore, the sum of these components somehow does not
add up to Botticelli's art because that art is a synthesis, and
not a sum. It is something which goes beyond any single element of his taste. It is the most intimate mark of his personality, of his creative power, impressing its character on
each element and making each element somehow new and
different. Besides fully appreciating the components of his
art in relation to their historical background, one must also

grasp the harmony of the whole of his creation, which while purely individual yet gives his art a universal value.

Figure 10 reproduces *The Virgin of the Grotto* by Leonardo da Vinci. The first impression we get from this painting is that the figures are no longer revealed against a background, but that the grotto itself is so painted as to seem actually to envelope the figures in the foreground. We have already seen in Pollaiuolo's picture the importance assigned to the landscape, but his figures always seem detached from the landscape. Leonardo's figures, on the contrary, are included in the landscape. Leonardo thoroughly realized the unity of human figures and their environment. With him the hierarchy of landscape and figures is reversed. A look at the paintings of Masaccio, Piero della Francesca and Botticelli is enough to convince us that the figures completely fill the space; they are the protagonists. In Leonardo's paintings it is the containing space which suggests the mood of the figures. They are therefore smaller and humbler. They are no longer the protagonists. They are, instead, merged with the whole. The rocks, as well as the figures, contribute to the expression of the whole.

The chiaroscuro, too, has changed. In Piero della Francesca, Pollaiuolo, and Botticelli the clear colors prevail against the shadows. Thus the plastic solidity of the figures is emphasized. Leonardo, on the contrary, increases the dark zones, with the result of softening the bodies and above all the contours. Pollaiuolo's chiaroscuro aims at a plastic detachment of the bodies. Leonardo's chiaroscuro aims at the immersion of the figures in the atmosphere of the picture. The protagonist is no longer the figure, but the chiaroscuro. The images, therefore, have no longer closed contours, but open forms; that is, open to the light and shadows outside the figures. Instead of plastic effect, Leonardo strives for pictorial effect. Contours fade away and bodies appear like atmospheric masses without the structural solidity usually associated with fifteenth-century Florentine art. This lessening of structural solidity has been considered by many critics as a weakness. It is not. Structural solidity is a necessity only for those painters who wish to realize it. But if Leonardo's ideal form is different, we have no right to require of him what he did not intend to offer. Leonardo's ideal was the nuance of chiaroscuro. If he had indulged in plastic structure he would have failed to show this nuance. But he fully realized his nuance and refused all other visual elements not in harmony with his ideal: thus, he was artistically right.

Pollaiuolo had found a relationship between anatomy and energy, which had a perfection of its own. Leonardo's drawings show that he knew anatomy even better than Pollaiuolo, but when he painted *The Virgin of the Grotto* he did not wish to show his knowledge of anatomy; neither did he wish to show his energy. Any sharp line, any intense movement, would have spoiled his nuance. He attained perfection in his painting because he absolutely fused all his elements into a delicate nuance.

Leonardo's mind was universal; he was painter, sculptor, architect, writer, and master of many sciences. And his writings show how subtle was his interest in color. Through his imagination he anticipated many color harmonies, common to us today, but ignored in his time. But in his painting he stayed clear of any variety of color-combinations, reducing all his colors to a nuance, almost to a monochrome, and insisting always on neutrals. For this he has often been wrongly reproached. But any artist has the right to approach his work the way he pleases in order to attain his objective. A *Virgin of the Grotto* painted in bright colors would have been an artistic absurdity.

The grandeur of Masaccio, the dignity of Piero della Francesca, the energy of Pollaiuolo, the grace of Botticelli were always expressed through a vivacious interest in man, as he is. Their individual ideal colored everything they accepted as reality, or immanent in reality. Leonardo, however, imagined an ideal transcending reality, an abstract ideal of grace. The twilight beyond the grotto, and the nuance of the figures' chiaroscuro have in common a silent grace.

This is the artistic aspect of Leonardo, not the story he tells. The scene in the picture shows the kneeling Madonna presenting the Child St. John to the Child Christ, for His blessing. An angel points his finger towards St. John to show him to Christ. This grouping of interrelated acts is quite unfortunate. The symbolism of these gestures, the artificiality of the grouping, of the angel looking towards the spectator to see if his beauty is recognized, the obviousness of pointing with his finger, the design of an action which concludes nothing, of a movement which is left in suspense, and finally, the structure which suggests a pattern without realizing it, all these aspects of the obvious expression of the group, offend by their lack of sentiment and by a too intricate, artificial composition.

But the art of Leonardo must not be sought in the sym-

58

bolism of a religious scene which is alien to his soul. His art must be sought instead, in his grace, in the nuance of his chiaroscuro. Here Leonardo himself helps us by his writings:

> Look at the faces of men and women on the streets when evening comes and the weather is bad; how great is the grace and sweetness one sees in them.

And, again:

> A body in half shadow will show very little difference between light and shade. This happens when evening comes or when it is cloudy. And if one paints such an effect, his work will be sweet and the faces will be graceful.

The nuance of a shadow was for Leonardo the ideal of beauty, grace, and perfection, and to it he sacrificed everything. Leonardo was born in 1452 in the little town of Vinci, near Florence. He died in France in 1519. He was steeped in the fifteenth-century Florentine tradition. In his early years he was influenced by Pollaiuolo, but soon found his own artistic bent. With an unswerving faith in the power of drawing he furthered the scientific knowledge of anatomy, engineering, aviation, mechanics, hydraulics, and many other fields of human endeavor. As a scientist he insisted on the revealing power of drawing, considering it an instrument of knowledge. But as a poet he not only felt the grace of the natural world about him but also found the connection between man and nature in half-tones and shadow. His artistic and scientific aims had the same origin—in the line. Later on, however, he discovered that the artistic world was different from the scientific one, and finally became convinced that the values of beauty, grace, etc., transcended factual reality. So

he adored nuance, and made of it his goddess. The transcendental was for him a form of escape from reality, which
he served mainly in his scientific research. But his poetry of
twilight was no escape. It was a very subtle perception of the
value of light and shade as prime factors in painting. Thus
he opened the way to the full pictorial ideal of modern times.
The fact that he realized his pictorial ideal through neutrals
rather than through the tonality of colors, does not, in any
way, detract from the recognition of an artistic perfection in
his paintings. He squandered all the wealth of color to live
in poverty with half-tones and shadows. But who can say
that the poor are less artistic than the rich? And who can deny
that the result of renouncing external beauty may sometimes
be the rediscovery of internal grace? This happened to Leonardo: and at this point we meet his eternal and absolute
art beyond his transient and relative preferences.

Chapter Three

Fig. 11. RAPHAEL: *The Sistine Madonna*, c. 1516.

Fig. 12. INGRES: *The Vow of Louis XIII*, 1824.

Fig. 13. RAPHAEL: *The School of Athens*, 1509-1511.

Fig. 14. PUVIS DE CHAVANNES: *Vision of the Antique*, 1885.

Chapter Three

THE IVORY TOWER

THE *Sistine Madonna* (fig. 11) is perhaps the most famous among the religious paintings of Raphael. And because Raphael is the most famous among the classic artists of the Renaissance, *The Sistine Madonna* has been considered the most perfect achievement in the classic style. However, if we wish to understand the art of Raphael, we must discount the enthusiasm lavished on it by so many generations of art lovers; we must discount all historical associations with that age of wonder known as the Renaissance, and forget the glory, which properly belongs outside the painting itself. In other words, it is necessary to look at this picture in the same way that we look at all other pictures, centering our attention on its particular type of formal expression rather than on external historical data.

The figures of this religious group appear through an open window, with opened curtains at the sides, and the parapet of the window shown at the base. The Madonna is shown descending from Heaven on a cloud bearing the Christ

Child in her arms towards the unseen faithful. On the left, and on a lower plane than the Madonna, Saint Sixtus, a pope, is kneeling on a cloud pointing out the faithful to the Child Christ for protection. On the right of the Madonna, St. Barbara, also kneeling on a cloud, is looking down towards the unseen earth. From the parapet two angels appear. The whole scene is at once a vision and a story. Let us begin with the vision.

In relation to the whole surface of the picture, the figures appear very large. The images painted by Piero della Francesca and Leonardo (figs. 7 and 10) are of a smaller proportion than those of *The Sistine Madonna*. The earth does not appear in Raphael's picture, which shows only two elements, the figures and the clouds, with the latter functioning as background. Also, the figures are shown in their mass and volume, with all details subordinated to the appearance of the masses. Thus both their proportions and the simplification of the forms result in an exceptional effect of grandiosity.

The ensemble of the figures is dark against a light background, that is, the effect is a pictorial and not a plastic one, which would require a light image against a dark background. However, Raphael's purpose is to give us the impression of a plastic effect, which is realized not in the ensemble, but only within the single figures, where the play of chiaroscuro emphasizes the round consistency of the bodies. The play of light in the picture does not depend on a single source. The light is very strong on the clear background, while the light falling on the figures remains unrelated to the background in order to stress the plastic effect. The light falling on the figures of the Madonna and Child comes from above, and from this group is deflected to the right side of St. Sixtus, and to the left side of St. Barbara. Thus there is an accord between plastic and pictorial effects, which is responsible for the solidity and the lightness of the figures. Their solidity is necessary for the monumental effect; while their lightness is necessary to justify their floating on the clouds. A similar accord exists between the structure and the pattern of the picture; the structure being revealed by the figures, and the pattern by the composition — which is a pyramid erected on a high rectangular base. And the same relationship exists between the surface and the depth of the picture; the whole composition being on the surface, while the volume of the figures suggests the occupation of a space in depth.

The whole composition is a static one. At each side of the vertical image of the Madonna, we see St. Sixtus and St. Barbara in a virtual symmetry — a symmetry which, however, is not fully materialized. In fact, the lower part of St. Sixtus extends below the left corner of the picture, while St. Barbara recedes on a higher level. We can even trace two parallel lines, one extending from the head of St. Sixtus to the head of the Madonna, and the other extending from the head of the left angel to the shoulder of St. Barbara. These lines are transversal, suggesting depth and the beginning of a movement. The movement is also suggested by the spiral lines which, starting from the mantle of the Madonna at her left elbow, continue around the left side of her body, and reach St. Barbara. This movement represents the fact that the Madonna is approaching the faithful from the sky. A perfect balance is therefore attained between the appearance of a static vision and the expression of a moving life.

63

This balance aims at convincing the spectator of the concrete reality of the figures, in spite of their appearing on
clouds. But there is an element in the picture which transcends reality and which constitutes Raphael's ideal. What
then is the nature of this ideal? Surely it is not to be found
in the religious character of the images, whether transcending
man or immanent in man. A comparison with the religious
characters painted by Giotto, Piero della Francesca, or Masaccio (figs. 1, 7, and 6) will soon convince us that the images
Raphael is portraying are very able actors rather than divine
or holy personages. The ideal of Raphael is beauty. The
glamor of the Madonna, the innocence of the children, the
picturesqueness of St. Sixtus, the self-conscious modesty of St.
Barbara, are varied aspects of his ideal of beauty.

By the time of Raphael classic culture had already become
widely diffused in Italy. He knew, therefore, that ideal beauty
in itself cannot be found in living creatures or in their repre-
sentations, but is to be found, instead, in geometrical figures. And Aristotle had confirmed the mathematical origin
of the beautiful. That is, an object to be beautiful had to
approach the regularity of geometrical forms. An ancient
Greek painter, Zeuxis, in order to portray an ideal beauty,
"inspected the maidens of the city naked, and chose five,
whose peculiar beauties he proposed to reproduce in his picture."[1] This legend means that Zeuxis did not believe in the
perfection of natural beauty, but that the artist ought to
choose from a variety of natural bodies those parts which,
combined, could produce an ideal beauty. Raphael recalled
this legend when he humorously wrote to his friend Bal-

[1]Cicero, *De Inventione*, II, II, 1-3.

dassare Castiglione: "In order to paint a beautiful woman, I should have to see many beautiful women, and have you with me to choose the best. But lacking both judges and beautiful women, I shall have to make use of a certain idea which I find in my mind." Raphael's own words give us to understand the transcending character of his idea of beauty and its relationship to natural bodies. The glamorized head of the Sistine Madonna is a great success. It represents Raphael's ideal perfection. From a social point of view, this Madonna belongs to the common people, not to the aristocracy; and by the very virtue of her belonging to a lower social class her idealized beauty rather than her natural beauty is emphasized. Her aristocracy depends on a principle much higher than that of class; it is the eternal aristocracy of beauty. The same must be said of the vitality of the children and of the rough old age of St. Sixtus. The expression of St. Barbara is too sweet and self-conscious for her beauty to be vital. But in the other figures we find a beauty enhancing vitality to an extent that it is very hard to find elsewhere.

The story itself as represented by *The Sistine Madonna* is less interesting. The Madonna does not express anything at all, human or divine, other than that she is the servant of God, who is a beautiful, powerful Child with a half-troubled, half-courageous countenance. St. Sixtus is an actor playing the rôle of patron of the faithful. The two angels are interested in the scene as spectators. And St. Barbara thinks much too highly of herself.

To devout people expecting of a religious painting the expression of a genuine religious impulse or moral passion, such a story shows not only indifference, but also vulgarity.

Both Giotto and Masaccio revealed through the human body a world of emotion. Piero della Francesca accentuated his ideal of human dignity and heroism. If one does not care for beauty *per se* he will not find in *The Sistine Madonna* anything but a show-window. But if he cares for this kind of beauty he will be richly rewarded, and will feel that this beauty has a strong vitality, and is an ideal form fused with reality.

These qualities are better understood if we compare Raphael's picture with *The Vow of Louis XIII* by Ingres (fig. 12). Here the Madonna, the curtains and clouds recall the Sistine Madonna. But all other elements appearing in this picture are Ingres's own invention. The composition includes a chapel, the curtains opened by the two angels, the altar below this group of figures, another pair of angels holding an inscription, and the King of France, Louis XIII, offering the Madonna his crown and scepter. The details are many, the separation of the upper part of the picture from the lower part is sharp, the transversal position of Louis XIII, who is depicted in depth, contrasts with the surface plane of the composition in the upper part of the picture. The visual unity perfectly realized by Raphael is broken up by Ingres. Raphael had a pictorial vision. He sought to integrate the unity of the whole composition by balancing the contrasting elements of figures and clouds. Ingres saw the group of the Madonna, the angels, Louis XIII, the altar and the clouds, separately; and then tried to unite them in a whirling pattern. He succeeded only partially. The Madonna, with dark tones, against the clear apsis, is certainly the best part of his picture. But Louis XIII is in part darker and in part lighter than the altar, thus hampering both the plastic and the pictorial effects. The painting of a vision calls for a static appearance, as is seen in the group of the Madonna, but the sharp action of Louis XIII does not belong to a vision. Statics and action are juxtaposed; they are described, but not visualized. Raphael saw reality even among the clouds; Ingres indulged in abstraction even on earth, and his overabundance of details transforms the vision into a scene of genre. Both Raphael and Ingres adored physical beauty. Ingres's Madonna with her perfect oval is very beautiful, but her geometric beauty is not alive. It lacks reality. Raphael's Madonna is essentially a portrait of a Roman girl idealized; Ingres's Madonna is a study of abstract beauty. What in Raphael is an imaginative creation, is in Ingres a demonstration of craftsmanship. Both paintings are lacking in religious feeling, but with this difference — that Ingres wants to serve the Catholic Church and the Kings of France; while Raphael serves only his ideal of beauty, which is not bound by historical limitations, but is in itself universal. No doubt Ingres painted beautiful forms, but to be art even beautiful forms need vitality and freedom of expression.

The School of Athens by Raphael (fig. 13) is a fresco painting on a wall of the Vatican Palace. Its purpose is to summarize the history of Greek philosophy. It is the most effective representation of the way the Italian people of the Renaissance conceived the intellectual life of the ancient Greeks. Here the story is of great importance, even if it is not the story of an action, but an exposition of a culture. The disposition of the figures draws the attention of the spectator to two figures standing in the center. They are Plato and Aristotle. Plato, an old man, points out the sky as a symbol of his idealistic philosophy. Aristotle, a realist, spreads out his hand towards the earth, a symbol of his realistic philosophy. They advance between two ranks of pupils, while other groups of philosophers and pupils are scattered about the place. On the left of Plato, a person, with a pug nose, arguing with his hands, is Socrates. Diogenes is lying on the steps in the middle foreground. In the foreground proper, at the left, is Pythagoras with his pupils; at the right are Euclid, the geometer, and Ptolemy and Zoroaster, the astronomers. Every image is alive with movement and interest in teaching or learning; and it is this very interest which gives life to the various attitudes of the characters shown in this picture without, however, showing action on their part. Raphael imagined the attitudes of his personages not only for the purpose of expressing their desire for learning, but also for the purpose of emphasizing the beauty of human bodies. Between the artist and his mode of expression there is this love of beauty for itself which constitutes the ideal of Raphael.

Of course, after the romantic trend of the nineteenth century, we are inclined to find a certain superficiality in this preoccupation with posturing. Thinking is for us too serious a matter to allow a thinker to play the rôle of an actor. But we must admit that a perfect balance between beautiful bodies and intellectual expression, as in *The School of Athens,* cannot be found elsewhere, either before or after Raphael. However, the artistic value of *The School of Athens* does not consist in Raphael's ability to characterize by the pose or

68

gesture of his figures the kind of thought the different philosophers of antiquity expressed. The exposition of a culture, in any form, does not reach the level of art, until an individual ideal is thereby expressed. The same thing applies to poetry: a summary of Greek philosophy is not a work of art, even if it be written in verse. And the balance between the various groups of figures, and their attitudes depicted in *The School of Athens* must not allow us to forget that this is a summary of Greek philosophy. Even the two gestures of Plato and Aristotle, aiming at the characterization of their respective philosophies, are a happy visualization of an idea, but such is neither poetry nor art. This is an important point in art criticism. The visualization of an idea has always something of a demonstration, a vulgarization of science. It is useful, it is interesting, no doubt, but it lacks that imaginative and emotional halo which is the necessary condition of art.

However, *The School of Athens* is a work of art, even a great work of art. It has that imaginative halo we spoke of. If one tries to understand what its artistic aspect is, he must forget the story, the summary of Greek philosophy, and center his attention on Raphael's imaginative vision. If the didactic center is the gesture of Plato and Aristotle, the artistic center is the background. How monumental are the arcades, one after the other in depth, with their ornaments of statues and reliefs! This architecture· is neither Greek nor Roman. It is the architecture of Raphael's friend, Bramante. To find his own reality Raphael sought the forms of his own time, outside the old Greek world. And how wide is the space where the Greek philosophers breathe! This spatial

69

magnitude expresses the ecstasy of Raphael before the heroes of an ancient civilization. It is this ecstatic mood which reveals the soul of Raphael, and which gives the figures something more than a physical beauty, something which transforms into a legend the summary of Greek philosophy. A unified rhythm—repeated in depth throughout the empty spaces of the arcades and throughout the space filled by the various groups of figures—expresses nobility, seriousness, and serenity born of an admiration for an ancient culture. Certainly such admiration is naïve. An archæologist of our time would smile at it. And science often smiles at the naïveté of the artistic imagination. But art is nourished by naïveté, by a childlike imagination soaring beyond the reaches of knowledge; there it finds its own realm. And the entire science of the world cannot substitute for it.

Puvis de Chavannes, too, had a vision of classical antiquity in the *Vision of the Antique* (fig. 14). It is not a summary of Greek philosophy, or of Greek art. His desire in this painting was to express that impalpable quality that was ancient Greek. Raphael's Greek philosophers argue, think, and teach. Puvis de Chavannes's Greek men and women are dreaming. Because ancient statues are often naked, Puvis de Chavannes's figures are more or less naked, too. His Greek landscape is full of rocks, bordering on the sea, with a blue sky like the permanent blue sky of ancient Hellas. There are goats, a goatherd with a syrinx, women at the well, some scattered trees and bushes, and in the middle distance a sculptor contemplating his Muse, while on the far distant shore we glimpse the prancing horses of the Parthenon. All this is

70

conventional archæology; that is, a reconstruction of Greece, not of a living Greece, but of a Greece existing only in a conventional erudition. This is not a poetic halo beyond reality, but a substitute for reality. A culture without life. The world of tedium. Raphael poetically expresses his ideal of a beautiful reality. Puvis de Chavannes conventionally portrays a will to poetry. He wishes his forms to be primitive, but succeeds only in rendering them primitivistic; that is, in escaping from a pictorial reality into intellectual schemes empty of emotion.

Poetry is form as well as content. To say that a painting is poetic, means that it has that free play of the imagination every art must have, and something more — an intimate delicacy, a nuancing of feeling which people attribute especially to poetry. Thus a poetic painting is one where visual form assumes an intimate delicacy.

But if a painter portrays a poet or a personage of a poem, for example a Muse, that does not mean that his subject matter will have a poetic value. Nobody will say that in *The School of Athens* Raphael did the work of a philosopher. For the same reason the subject matter of Puvis de Chavannes does not determine the poetic value of his picture. The conventional knowledge the painter had of ancient Greece hampered, rather than furthered, the realization of his imaginative vision. He painted archæological schemes, abstracted from a past Greek reality as well as from his own feeling. It is an intellectual game without any serious emotion.

This is a problem in art criticism which goes beyond Puvis de Chavannes's painting. Painters and critics alike in recent

71

times have condemned the poetic in painting, and have justified their condemnation by stressing the distinction between poetry and painting. But poems and paintings are works of art, and find their common ground in the artistic attitude of imagination, expression, and experience. A poet is a painter in words, and a painter is a poet in visual forms. The artistic mistake begins when a poet describes what he sees without emotion, or a painter portrays poetic motives without visual sensibility. In such cases we have neither poets nor painters, but people who try to appear gifted with poetic or visual talent which they do not possess. They are false to themselves and to others, and are excluded from the realm of art.

Raphael (1483–1520) was born in the little town of Urbino. He received his early education in the provincial town of Perugia, and later in the artistic capital of Italy, Florence. He was inspired by both Leonardo da Vinci and Michelangelo. From his immediate predecessors and contemporaries he assimilated the best means of attaining beauty. The Florentine tradition cared little for beauty in itself. What it was primarily concerned with was the understanding of moral and physical reality rather than beauty. But what for the Florentines was an aim, was for Raphael only a means. His aim was beauty. And because physical beauty flatters the vanity of mankind, the success of Raphael was tremendous, lasting throughout the centuries to our own day. He was a naturally gifted individual who attained his artistic aim with great natural ease. He transformed all the elements assimilated from other painters into something new and unexpected with such perfect harmony that even what he assimilated from others became his own. The ease of his extraordinary results suggested that he had a divine gift.

All this could not have happened without a profound desire to escape from reality. At the beginning of the sixteenth century Italian politics were at the edge of an abyss, and the Italian people for three centuries lost both their freedom and their independence. The Catholic Church was on the point of receiving from the Reformation the most terrific setback in her long history. Foreign armies pouring into Italy destroyed the civilization of the Renaissance. To lose oneself in beauty meant to escape, or at least to delude oneself with the sense of escaping, from earthly troubles. Beauty was a goddess, perhaps the only one Italians could then adore. Think of Giotto, Masaccio, Piero della Francesca, or Pollaiuolo — certainly their artistic ideal was not an ideal of beauty for itself. Even Botticelli and Leonardo cared more for grace than for physical beauty; grace to them being a more subtle and spiritual quality than beauty. This then must mean that beauty can be an ideal of art, but is not, however, the only ideal of art. We realize this truth more forcefully when we become aware that in the last hundred years the best artists have cared very little for beauty. Beauty, therefore, must be considered a possible condition of art essential to some artists, but non-essential to others.

Beauty became the necessary condition of Raphael's art because of his desire to escape the troubles of his time. He found beauty in an ivory tower and thus initiated the trend towards "art for art's sake." Every work of art is an autonomous entity reflecting the life and personality of its creator, but with a life of its own. Therefore artistic activity must be distinguished from scientific, moral, and religious activity. But to be distinguished does not mean to be detached: art is a human activity and cannot be completely detached from other human activities. What distinguishes art from other activities is the result, the definite form, of the work of art. But the process of creation, and the matter that the artist must transform, must embrace the whole of human life where scientific, moral, and religious activities have their place. If we completely isolate artistic creation from all other activities we have a form without content, a game and not a serious engagement, and we finally arrive at "art for art's sake" — an art so purified and so abstract as to lose all the quality of art. Then an artist ceases to be an artist and becomes a subtle technician, a virtuoso, an academician, and his art becomes an academic art devoid of all content.

No doubt Raphael was the founder of academic art, but he himself is not an academician. His creation of the glamorous beauty of *The Sistine Madonna,* or of the exalting spaces of *The School of Athens,* was accompanied by such a naïve joy in their serenity and beauty that the emotional quality necessary to art was not lacking, even if it was somewhat rarefied.

His followers throughout the centuries — and these can be counted by the thousands — saw in Raphael's paintings only the beautiful forms and not the emotion which had prompted their creation. These followers repeated or modified them with a cold heart, and with a studious intellect. They even tried to perfect them through intellectual refinements, without being aware that their work, as Ruskin said, was like "the watering of trees whose stems are cut through."

Ingres (1780–1867) and Puvis de Chavannes (1829–98)

74

were academic painters in the full sense of the word. Both believed in, or at least painted, forms abstracted from life and therefore lifeless. Ingres was faithful to the ideal of Raphael's form, which he considered the perfection of art. But there is no absolute perfection in art. Raphael's form was a perfection relative to Raphael. To believe, as Ingres did, that only through Raphael's form could he attain his own artistic perfection meant that Ingres renounced the possibility of his own artistic perfection. Ingres's best paintings were mostly portraits, where the reality of the sitter obliged the painter to modify that form he believed perfect. We may even say that in a painter like Ingres only his shortcomings, his imperfections, are artistic.

However, the problem of Puvis de Chavannes is more complex. He was not any one man's devotee. His dream was of a primitive form, older than Raphael's, approaching Greek archaic sculpture. But he was as far from primitive Greek sensibility as a nineteenth-century contemporary of Impressionist painters could possibly be. His leaning towards Greek taste was wishful thinking, and his pretension to Greek taste blinded him to the actuality around him. The result was a gathering of lifeless schemes which he tried in vain to justify by decorating walls instead of painting canvases.

At this point it is necessary to state that a painting executed in fresco on a wall has no claim to be judged differently from one painted in oil on a canvas. Both should be judged by the same artistic standard. Unfortunately, in recent times the fashionable painting of murals has confused many a critical mind. What would have been considered academic if painted on a canvas was justified as a mural. But a lifeless

75

form remains lifeless even if it be repeated a hundred times on a wall. And today the conception of form has become so complicated and difficult, because of its richness, that it is impossible to multiply forms by the hundreds without reducing them to the lowest level. To call murals decorative works does not necessarily prove that they are artistic. A still-life by Cézanne is an artistic decoration. But to cover a wall with the lifeless schemes of Puvis de Chavannes does not mean that the decoration will be artistic. In other words, decoration is a function which can be fulfilled by both artistic and non-artistic works. And to be artistic, a decoration must have the same qualities as all other works of art—qualities of imagination, expression, and experience.

Chapter Four

THE DISCOVERY OF NATURE

IN THE fifteenth century, Florentines discovered man. They analyzed his physical structure, his emotional nature, his various mental attitudes and moral ideals towards life, his place in space, his proportions and his relation to geometric forms, his capability of movement and action, and finally his relation to his natural surroundings. Their aim was concentrated in man, the center of the universe.

A Venetian painter, Giorgione, who died very young (*c.* 1480–1510), directed his attention toward a new goal. He concentrated his attention on nature, and conceived human beings as no longer the center of the universe, but as simple elements of the universe. Thus, he discovered nature for the art of painting.

The source of this change which modified the whole course of modern taste must be found principally in his own feelings. He worshiped nature, with a deeper feeling for nature than all his contemporaries. He loved trees, rivers, sky, and

77

loving them he impressed them with his own human life. Personalizing them, he made them human beings, and by their harmonious wholeness they acquired a dignity of their own and expressed human feeling.

Besides Giorgione's artistic feeling, certain conceptual and visual trends also concurred in this change of taste.

Leonardo da Vinci theorized about a painting able to represent the whole universe; that is, a painting where not only man but everything in nature, from a raindrop to the stars, could be represented. But his actual paintings, however, failed very much to carry out his universal conception. The philosophers of the University of Padua, where Venetian culture was founded, made early researches into the physical properties of nature without much concern for man. Theirs was a first attempt at a philosophy of nature.

On the other hand, Venetian painters of the fifteenth century paid more attention to coloring than their Florentine contemporaries. From the Florentine painters they learned about the new discoveries concerning the human form, perspective and anatomy, but their own application of these new discoveries to the art of painting always bore an original and conscious quality of coloring.

The accent on nature and on coloring converged in the artistic feeling of Giorgione, and a new era of imaginative painting was born. The composition of figures had been until then used principally for the purpose of telling a story, religious in Giotto and in Masaccio, and mythological in Pollaiuolo. Botticelli did not tell a story in his *Spring,* but presented figures for their own sake. However, some poets had provided him with motives, as religion did with Leo-

Fig. 15. GIORGIONE: *The Thunderstorm*, c. 1505.

Fig. 16. TITIAN: *The Temptation of Adam and Eve,* 1565-70.

Fig. 17. MICHELANGELO: *The Temptation of Adam and Eve,* 1508-10.

Fig. 18. TITIAN: *Christ Crowned with Thorns*, 1570–71.

Fig. 19. EL GRECO: *The Pentecost*, c. 1606.

nardo and Raphael. But every one realizes that if a painter paints a tree instead of a human figure he cannot tell a story at all, or his story is reduced within narrow limits. Giorgione indeed deliberately renounced story-telling, even when he imagined compositions of figures. Art critics in the sixteenth century were shocked by the fact that they could not understand what Giorgione had represented. But we in the twentieth century are not shocked at all, because we know the difference between the subject matter and the content of a picture. And we realize that Giorgione, by focusing his attention on nature, naturally avoided all story-telling, and in so doing attained a greater freedom in expressing both content and form.

Look at Giorgione's *Thunderstorm* (fig. 15). In this painting human figures don't act; they have no relation to each other; they are part of nature, and like trees, houses, and water, simply live under the menace of nature. If there is a residue of a story it is certainly not the figures but the landscape, with the lightning in the sky, that tells it. However, this residue is so small that we can ignore it, and believe that there is no story at all. This disappearance of the story from painting had the utmost importance in the history of human taste in painting. The unity of form and content is thus completely achieved and emphasized. And just as the lyric is the expression only of the feeling of the poet, so the lyrical value of a painting without a story becomes more apparent. As an expression of sentiment, every real work of art has a lyrical value, but if this lyrical value has to be revealed through a story its manifestation is bound to be more complex and possibly distorted, sometimes losing its effectiveness.

79

In *The Thunderstorm* the background assumes the rôle of the protagonist in the scene. Menacing clouds are gathering; a streak of lightning tears them asunder. It is just at sunset and the light falls on the houses along a canal. The canal is dark, as is the sky, and both serve to frame the brilliant, almost mottled light reflected on the houses. An unnatural light, a light which is precious and smiling, but at the same time uncertain and suggestive of its own passing. The foreground is separated from the menacing storm and the melancholy light by an old ruin and a group of trees, forming a kind of grove for the protection of the gypsy and the soldier who are participating in the cosmic life of nature. They are as calm as the water flowing over rocks and meadows. Wordsworth defined the lyric as "emotion, recollected in tranquillity." This painting is an example of such lyrical poetry, dedicated to the approaching sunset behind the thunderstorm and to the shelter men and things find in a secluded corner of the countryside withdrawn from the active world.

When we spoke of Leonardo's painting we emphasized the fact that his images were immersed in the atmosphere thus avoiding that isolation from the surrounding nature which previous Florentine painters had preferred. But the realization of Leonardo's figures immersed in the atmosphere was due to nuances of chiaroscuro, that is, to neutral colors. He completely disregarded the qualities of colors, thus reducing his paintings almost to monochromes.

Giorgione, on the contrary, loved colors, intense colors. We have spoken of the intensity of color of Simone Martini, who loved gemlike colors and harmonized them with a gold background. But Simone Martini never intended to use his in-

tense qualities of color to suggest light and shade. After
a century during which the subject of chiaroscuro was
widely studied, Giorgione himself could not but be concerned
with the relation between light effects and the qualities of
colors. So he struck a balance between his intense sense of
colors and their function as light and shade in a picture.
That is, he used one color to suggest light and one to suggest
shadow. This is the principle of tonality in painting. Thus
Giorgione opened the way for all the effects of light and
shade instead of chiaroscuro. Chiaroscuro being the technique
of plastic form, tonality became, with Giorgione, the perfect
technique of pictorial form.

Now think of a figure isolated from its natural environment: the revealing quality about it is its intimate structure.
But if a figure is seen through lights and shadows reflected
from the outside world, then that figure is no longer isolated;
it becomes an element of the universe revealed by light and
shade. Giorgione stressing colors as functions of light and
shade conceived the character of his form as a consequence
of his nuances of tonality instead of chiaroscuro. This kind
of form due to tonality is the *pictorial form*.

Through his love of nature, humanization of nature, and
visualization of form as light and shade, Giorgione reached
a perfect unity of content and form. The delicacy he saw in
the human figure, the poetic synthesis he brought to the
elements of a landscape, their lyrical and idyllic rendering,
together with their intensity of physical life — all these were
the consequence of Giorgione's unity of form and content.
At the very moment when Raphael was retiring to his ivory
tower in search of beauty, Giorgione was broadening his

human interest to embrace the whole of nature. His discovery of his own sense of beauty was at the same time a discovery of a new reality in painting.

Although Giorgione died at the age of thirty his work opened the eyes of Titian, a schoolmate of Giorgione, to the new horizon in painting. Titian (1477–1576) then became the leader of Venetian painters, renewing his style after 1550 (at about seventy years of age), towards the freest pictorial ideal ever known — an ideal which became a model for the best painting of the following three centuries.

To understand the difference between the Venetian and the Florentine conception of form it would be useful to compare two paintings with the same subject matter, *The Temptation of Adam and Eve:* one by Titian (fig. 16) and one by Michelangelo (fig. 17).

Michelangelo's conception of form was based on his knowledge of anatomy. In his *Temptation of Adam and Eve,* he painted the man and the woman in strong relief, giving them the appearance of statues in the round, instead of the appearance of pictorial figures. This was due to his use of chiaroscuro instead of real color. And the gestures of his figures were freely interpreted and clearly rendered in order to attain a plastic realization of their movement. From the anatomical structure of the figures flows their inner construction, around which the surfaces of their body are extended, and which has the function of showing the movement. Here, as in all his paintings, the aim of Michelangelo is not merely that of showing the action or the form of a body, but of finding a unity of movement which goes beyond the unity of action.

82

The woman ending in a snake is shown giving the forbidden apple to Eve while Adam helps the action by lowering the branch of the Tree of Knowledge. The composition of the three figures, Adam, Eve, and the woman-snake, is strictly enclosed within a clear pattern and finds a perfect equilibrium. The vision of Michelangelo does not go from nature to human figures, nor from the surface of things to their structure; it starts with the anatomical structure of bodies and expands outward to their surface, movement, and action. The process of creation is thus from the inside outward — from what Michelangelo knows to what he sees.

The process in Titian is the very opposite one — from the outside inward. What he sees first is the mass, not the structure. For example, in his picture *The Temptation of Adam and Eve,* the color of Eve's body is clearer than that of Adam. And the pivot of the whole composition is a tree, which separates the two bodies. The bodies are treated in the same way as the trees; they are in effect masses of colors. The values of the bodies are shown for themselves, not for their movement. True, some action is shown: Eve is shown taking the apple from the snake, symbolized by the body of a child, while Adam tries to stop Eve. But this action lacks the movement and the plastic evidence of Michelangelo's figures. The movement is merely a pretext to show the glamorous body of Eve and the robust body of Adam. Movement in itself has very little importance in Titian's picture. These bodies are not detached from their surrounding nature, as in Michelangelo. They belong to nature. Their characteristic is not anatomy or chiaroscuro but mass, more or less clearly rendered. Their contours are not closed as in Michelangelo, but open, as though merging with the atmosphere of their natural surroundings. The difference lies in the fact that Michelangelo aims at plasticity, and Titian at volumes. Volumes are pictorial masses, as distinguished from plastic reliefs.

Titian's figures are much more truly representative of a real man and woman than are those of Michelangelo, who went beyond reality in order to find a more abstract rhythm and a more ideal proportion. If Titian's Eve is a real woman, Michelangelo's Eve is a heroine, strong as a man. On the other hand, if Titian's Adam, done in color tones, is a robust man, Michelangelo's Adam, through the subtleties of his chiaroscuro, becomes weak in comparison.

The difference between the styles of Michelangelo and Titian is emphasized even more by their different conception of coloring. The qualities of a painting for Michelangelo are reason, symmetry, proportion, intelligence, choice, solidity, and energy. He wants sculpture to be his guide in painting. A white statue does not require color for its artistic effect. Thus, in painting, Michelangelo uses color only as a function of chiaroscuro, without any interest in color for itself. He conceives form through his imagination rather than sensing it through color.

In this connection it is necessary to define precisely what we mean by form. Again, a comparison with poetry will prove useful. From the beginning of our analysis we have made a distinction between the form and the content of a poem. Art being a synthesis of form and content, form must be considered essential to any poem which claims to be a real work of art. If we analyze the form of Michelangelo as distinct from his content, we find that the content is the proportioned solidity that Michelangelo imparts to a form by virtue of which it becomes an artistic form. The same process goes on in Titian, thereby imparting an artistic form to a content which represents his prosperous and energetic life.

But another meaning of form is also assumed in painting —a meaning which no longer makes a distinction between form and content, but between form and color. Michelangelo realized form through plastic effects; Titian through color effects. Both are artistic forms. An erroneous tradition of criticism confuses artistic form as distinguished from content, and plastic form as distinguished from color. This tradition is an erroneous one because it considers plastic form as an essential element of art. The truth is that if artistic form is necessary to all works of art, plastic form is necessary to some works of art and not to others. Color, too, has become an artistic form in painting. And if some painters conceive a motif under chromatic form, and insist on plastic form, they hinder their artistic result instead of helping it. For example, Titian conceiving a chromatic form submitted his plastic form to a composition in colors, and his result was color-volumes, and not plasticity. Conversely, Michelangelo conceiving plastic form submitted his coloring to his plasticity, and the result was plastic forms, not color-volumes.

Therefore we cannot say that Michelangelo's form is better than Titian's. Both Michelangelo and Titian have a perfect artistic form as the result of two different choices of elements in painting—Michelangelo stressing plasticity and Titian coloring. And because artistic form is essential to any work of art, it is a quality without which there can be no art. But plastic form is not essential to all artists, at all times. It depends on the individual artist's preference, which changes, and has changed, with different artists and at different historical periods. It is not a quality which art criticism should consider necessary to its judgment of values. Chromatic volumes also depend on the individual artist's preference. We cannot praise a painting because it has plastic form, or another because of its chromatic form. Artistic form uses plasticity or volumes; both are means and not results. The result depends on how plasticity or volumes have been used. It is the coherent harmony of all the elements in a painting which determines whether plasticity or volumes were used correctly or not. These two pictures by Michelangelo and Titian show this perfect coherence, both therefore have a perfect artistic form.

To understand Michelangelo's art, a comparison with Masaccio (fig. 6) and Pollaiuolo (fig. 8) may be useful. Masaccio, too, attained a perfect plastic form through chiaroscuro. However, Masaccio's chiaroscuro appears simpler than that of Michelangelo. The latter produced a greater fluency of movement. The anatomical structure of Masaccio's figures is perfect, but much less apparent than that of Michelangelo's figures. On the other hand, the life-giving energy and the intensity of expression are much greater in Masaccio's work. Michelangelo has a rhythm of forms, a fluency of movement, a natural development of surfaces, and finally a sense of grandeur which are not so evident in Masaccio.

Now let us carry our comparison farther. In Pollaiuolo's Hercules the anatomy is stressed even more than in Michel-

86

angelo's work, with accentuated lines which emphasize the energy of its movement, but hinder the grace which is so evident in Michelangelo's figures. And which depends for its effect on the nuances of chiaroscuro and the development of surfaces.

Thus Michelangelo's work is much more abstract than most of the paintings done in the Florentine tradition of the fifteenth century. He imagined plastic form detached from its natural surroundings as well as from human reality. But because his vision of a heroic world as distinct from the actual, material, and moral one is ideally perfect and imaginatively coherent, his result is vital even if breathing in a rarefied atmosphere. It is a world where people are more majestic than people on earth, and move with an intimate dignity, certainty, ease, and solidity. Michelangelo chose chiaroscuro, movement, and grandeur to represent human forms and the visual world and ignored the other elements of vision, but he superbly realized the intimate agreement of these elements, thus attaining a majestic perfection all his own.

Michelangelo Buonarroti (1475–1564) was the most influential artist working towards an ideal of sculptural monumentality, even in painting. It was a classic ideal, realized above all in his nude figures; and it was considered an unsurpassed perfection. In his ideal, Michelangelo belonged to the same ivory tower we spoke of when we studied Raphael. But Michelangelo's temperament did not agree with his ideal —he was a moral and religious man who felt very deeply the tragedy of Italy and its loss of freedom, and in spite of his principles he could not help but reflect in his work his sense of tragedy and restless energy, which went beyond his own ideal of form and opened the way to new forms in art.

The ideal of Titian was different from that of Michelangelo. Following the youthful dream of Giorgione, Titian was able throughout his long life to lead all the Venetian painters of the sixteenth century towards a vision of human figures whereby both man and nature participated on an equal footing. He did not seek, in supernatural spheres, beauty, grace, monumentality as qualities in his painting, but within nature itself. And he could realize his purpose because he had at his disposal a much greater tradition of coloring than the Florentines.

In a *Dialogue on Painting* by Ludovico Dolce, published in 1557, we read: "The principal part of coloring is the contrast of light and shade. And that is the medium which enables the two elements to agree in order to give figures an effect of roundness and their right placement, near or far. Some people paint flesh so colored and so hard that it seems made of porphyry; its shades are too dark and sometimes they end in being pure black. Some artists paint flesh too white, some too red. I prefer a coloring of flesh quite brown, rather than too white. Above all one must not think that coloring consists in the choice of beautiful colors, like fine reds, blues, or greens. I believe that a certain neglect is necessary because coloring must not be too charming nor figures too completely finished: in every part one must see a gentle firmness. The greatest danger is to be too diligent."

Dolce portrays in words some of the qualities of Titian's art. Between light and shadow an intermediate color is invented: the brownish tone. The properties of things, whether flesh, wood, metal, are reproduced by the different reactions of light to each material. Colors are no longer appreciated for their individual beauty, but for their amalgamation into a general effect of light and shadow. Contours are open, instead of closed, in order to continue the masses of color, called volumes, into the surrounding atmosphere through which light passes. Open contours give figures the aspect of being unfinished. They are *unfinished* only relatively to the closed contours of the Florentines. But with the open contours of the Venetians they are perfectly finished figures: thus this unfinished quality is the perfect *finish* of pictorial form. This *pictorial finish* is an affirmation of freedom from a too diligent craftsmanship in order to distinguish the free wandering of artistic imagination from the excessive diligence of artisanship. Because of open contours and this pictorial finish, the vibration of light gives a cosmic vibration to any image, suggesting a continuous movement in any figure, whether seated or lying. All this constitutes the innovation and the perfection of Titian's style.

The difference in visualization between the Venetians and the Florentines has been interpreted since the sixteenth century as Venetian realism against Florentine idealism. As we have already pointed out, the conquest of different aspects of reality grew always more complex from Giotto to Leonardo. Florentine humanism was a way to reality, an impulsion towards the understanding of reality. Venetians enlarged enormously this field of reality and it is only natural that such an enlargement was considered by them as the whole of reality. This was an illusion; every new discovery in painting is an addition of some aspect of reality to those already known. Venetians, too, were idealists in their own way. Dignity, solemnity, monumentality are qualities as inherent in Titian's style as in Michelangelo's.

The Florentine Renaissance was a popular creative movement towards a fuller life. Artists went beyond this popular current only through their æsthetic ideals. But by the time Titian's style had matured, something had happened which modified the whole of Italian life. This was the Spanish conquest of Italy, partial in fact, but general as to social life. Spaniards brought to Italy ceremonial forms, a consciousness of nobility, an external decorum, which they had inherited from feudalism and which appeared as a sign of power and grandeur. The "sosiego," or impassive solemnity, was the social form reflecting Spanish psychology. Titian, shrewd, like a peasant, in his business dealings and simple in his social relations, became the painter of the Emperor, Charles V, and his court. There he admired the solemnity, the richness, the aristocratic expression of the great Spaniards. And his style bears the mark of his admiration. The relationship between Italian popular creativeness and the "sosiego" ideal was mediated by this new kind of social courtesy. It was a social ideal and it, too, became a new aspect of reality in painting.

Titian's *The Temptation of Adam and Eve* is an excellent example of his normal form, but he sometimes went much farther in the development of his style.

His *Christ Crowned with Thorns* (fig. 18) is a milestone in his conception of light. A distinction, however, must be made here between *universal* and *particular* light. In the open country during the day the light is universal: it moulds a human body and envelops it. Even the shadows do not conceal any part of the body, but rather complement the effect

90

of light, emphasizing the plasticity of the body. But if a lamp
is brought into a dark room the light does not envelop everything; it reveals one spot and conceals another. No figure
can be completely illuminated, nor completely seen. There
is no longer the form of a figure, but only certain details
revealed by the light while other details are lost in the darkness. In other words, the parts of a figure which are illuminated suggest the other parts in the darkness which are
not seen but imagined. This is the effect of particular light.
The artist who paints a particular light does not center his
attention on the figures. His purpose is not to present figures,
but effects of light.

Furthermore, a plastic figure must have some weight perceived by intuition, and its movement will always be limited
by its weight. But light, being incorporeal, is a vibration and
therefore always in movement. A particular light has the
rapidity of lightning: it touches and reveals, then it disappears. That is, it gives movement even to seated figures
and emphasizes action as well as movement.

When we looked at Pollaiuolo's Hercules (fig. 8) we said
that his movement was only the stance of a movement. This
meant expression of movement through lines. But in Titian's
Christ Crowned with Thorns the movement is evidenced by
the coincidence of action and light. The particular light thus
emphasizes the stress of action. Pollaiuolo's structure was
based on anatomy; but the structure of Titian's figures and
of his whole composition depends entirely on light.

To speak of an action in painting is always metaphorical.
Actually, there are in painting only the illusions of action, but
never action itself. And those painters who aimed at repro-

ducing real action went outside the field of art because they reduced art to reality. Art is not created to deceive people — deception being the province of artifice. Many legends tell us of certain curtains painted so well that a visitor tried to open them. Those painted curtains were not works of art. But if the impression of an action is produced by an effect of light, then light becomes the form of the action, which has found its own artistic expression. And instead of being deceived, the spectator contemplates the effect of light, which is art itself.

In both Michelangelo's and Titian's versions of *The Temptation of Adam and Eve* their plastic bodies or volumes are revealed in the foreground. But in Titian's *Christ Crowned with Thorns* the composition follows a diagonal line from the right foreground to the left background so that the images occupy space in depth. Instead of the juxtaposition of the figures, as in Botticelli's *Spring* (fig. 9), there is in this painting by Titian a superimposition of figures so that they appear foreshortened and only partially revealed. We have already noted how a particular light reveals some part of an object directly in the path of the light while it conceals others; thus both the type of the composition and of the lighting in the *Christ Crowned with Thorns* are homogeneous. And the unity of visualization is perfect.

The physical beauty of a figure is seen only when the figure is shown in its entirety. Titian's Eve is a beautiful figure. But there are no beautiful figures in *Christ Crowned with Thorns*. What, then, was the æsthetic purpose of Titian when he painted this picture? The disorder of brutality and violence manifested around the resigned nobility of the suffering Christ reveals a dramatic contrast which has a moral and not a physical beauty. Moral beauty is in this case a synonym for the dramatic expression of light.

The Venetian principle of *particular light* proved very fruitful. Titian's drama in *Christ Crowned with Thorns* was conceived on earth as a moral struggle between brutality and nobility. But imagine the same principle adopted by a painter who used reality only as a springboard towards mystical transcendency, and you meet Domenikos Theotocopoulos, known as El Greco.

In Titian's paintings light assumed the function of the structure around which figures are developed, and in spite of their subordination to light they retain their own physical and moral individuality so that one can distinguish the old man from the young man, the brutal executioner from the noble Victim. Not only that, but through the variety of the design the movement of the composition is subtly harmonized with the action in the picture.

Figure 19 represents *The Pentecost* by El Greco. Here light not only functions as the structure but is the whole form of the picture. A series of flames burns over the heads of the figures, and each figure in turn assumes the form of a flame. A few figures are seated, most of them are not. But all of them are caught up in their own emotional frenzy by the revelation from Heaven. And all of them vibrate with a unique kind of intense vibration. It is a kind of dance, not of bodies, but of lights. A mystical dance which lifts incorporeal images towards the dove of the Holy Spirit. El Greco's expression of this mystical revelation is not realized through human figures but through this vibration of light. The gestures of the figures are arbitrary and fail to express the emotional content of El Greco's experience. If one wants to understand this painting he must look not at the figures but at the radiation of light. For the same reason the unnatural lengthening of the figures is as arbitrary as a form for the figures as it is necessary and fortunate as the form of the lights. This elongation has been one of the greatest obstacles to the understanding of El Greco's art. One never sees in real life men and women with such elongated proportions. But this fact has nothing to do with the quality of art. No one has ever seen a tree with the form of a column, but a column can be a work of art. And there is no æsthetic principle which forbids in painting what it admits in architecture. Some physicians have written books trying to explain El Greco's approach to art by an illness in the man: a very foolish assumption by people who do not know what they are talking about, because, while speaking of art, what they are actually doing is passing judgment on a physical reality. If art is a product of the free play of the imagination it is the coherence of the imagination, and not a common reality, which one must try to understand. Titian is a realist, but one will never in one's own experience of reality come upon such a scene as is found in *Christ Crowned with Thorns*. The main difference between these two artists is that El Greco's imagination is much more abstract than Titian's. But a greater or less detachment from reality is no measure for artistic judgment.

Only in the historical development of El Greco's style can we find the intimate reason for it. El Greco (1541–1614) was born in Crete, where he became saturated with the

Byzantine style, which shunned the study of reality in favor of conventional forms. From Crete he went to Venice, where he gained the most advanced knowledge of light and coloring from Titian. From Venice he went to Rome, where he became acquainted with the prevailing mannerism of making use of the conventional forms inspired by Michelangelo's monumental style. From Rome he finally drifted to Toledo, where Saint Teresa had already created a mystical center. The use of light and coloring learned in Venice became the means for interpreting reality, and in his portraits El Greco demonstrates how aware he was of realistic values. But when reality was no longer the content of his coloring, he foresaw that the mystical impulse experienced in Toledo could substitute for reality and become the matter of transcendency. This mystical experience was responsible for his exasperating coloring — which reached new horizons of daring harmony — uniting in burning flames all the elements of his painting.

Conventional forms in themselves are not expressive of anything and cannot give life to works of art. But in El Greco, conventional forms are simply a means of realizing lights and colors. That is, in his painting, there are no longer conventional forms in themselves. There are only lights and colors revealing by their own power the mystical content of his message. And so we have no right to ask him for forms of figures if he wants to offer us the expression of his lights and colors instead.

It is indeed a rare day for humanity when a painter with such a powerful imagination as El Greco assimilates and harmonizes so many different elements of taste as the Byzantine, the Venetian, the Roman, and the Spanish. We owe

95

to his creative power the demonstration that the whole experience of art in the Renaissance could be used not only for the interpretation of reality, but for the expression of a mystical transcendency. Thus he enriched to the utmost the possibility of the expression of light and color, divorced from the experience of reality. Since El Greco's art is an abstract art, and therefore little understood, it was despised for two centuries. However, in the nineteenth century it was rediscovered, and today it is more than ever exalted.

Chapter Five

THE IDEAL VALUES OF LUMINISTIC
REALISM

Fig. 20. CARAVAGGIO. The Call of St. Matthew

Fig. 21. REMBRANDT. The Supper in Emmaus

Fig. 22. REMBRANDT. Portrait of Himself

Fig. 23. TITIAN. Portrait of Jacopo da Strada

Fig. 24. RAPHAEL. Portrait of a Cardinal

Fig. 25. VELASQUEZ. The Child of Vallecas

THE CHANGE in taste in art from Giotto to El Greco followed a nexus of various directions which were homogeneous in character. Their trend was towards a lyrical unity, towards an expression of sentiment as immediate and pure of details as it could possibly be. In Giotto and in Piero della Francesca one finds statements of single facts that cannot be found in the later Titian or in El Greco. One can explain the difference by saying that the components of Giotto's style were coordinated with one another, and that the components of El Greco's style were subordinated to the predominating one — namely light. In other words, the most important trend in painting from the fourteenth century to the end of the sixteenth century was the conquest in the expression of feeling at the sacrifice of the representation of factual statements.

Of course this trend was not a continuous one. From time to time certain pauses were necessary to stress statements, and as the springboard for new journeys towards expression. Portraits, for example, were always a welcome opportunity for keeping in touch with facts, that is, with the likeness of the sitter which was often remote both from ideal beauty and the feeling of the artist. However, at the end of the sixteenth century a reaction set in which stressed the statement of facts in painting, and which was epitomized by Caravaggio. A name was found for that reaction: realism. The majority of Western painters from Giotto on aimed at the interpretation of nature. But Caravaggio's realism was something new because of his polemical character, which was both artistic and social.

But what is realism in art? A work of art is at once an impression of reality and an expression of the soul; it is both real and ideal. The distinction between realistic and idealistic painters can only be relative. Some artists concentrate on the portrayal of what they see and feel when confronted with an object of reality; others consider their impression of reality the starting point for their imagination, which can then proceed autonomously to the limit of its possibilities. Both approaches belong to the realm of art unless they stop too short, or go too far. If a realistic painter to be objective represents every detail of reality without selection and without expressing his sentiment towards the reality which he reproduces, he becomes photographic, and his work fails as far as art is concerned. If an idealistic painter goes so far in the realm of

Fig. 20. CARAVAGGIO: *The Call of St. Matthew*, c. 1592

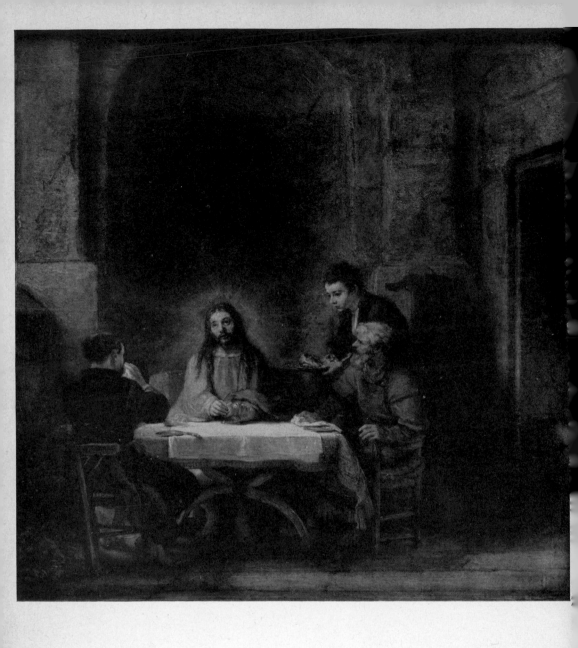

Fig. 21. REMBRANDT: *The Supper in Emmaus*, 1648.

Fig. 22. REMBRANDT: *Portrait of Himself,* c. 1663.

Fig. 23. TITIAN: *Portrait of Jacopo da Strada*, 1568.

Fig. 24. RAPHAEL: *Portrait of a Cardinal*, c. 1511.

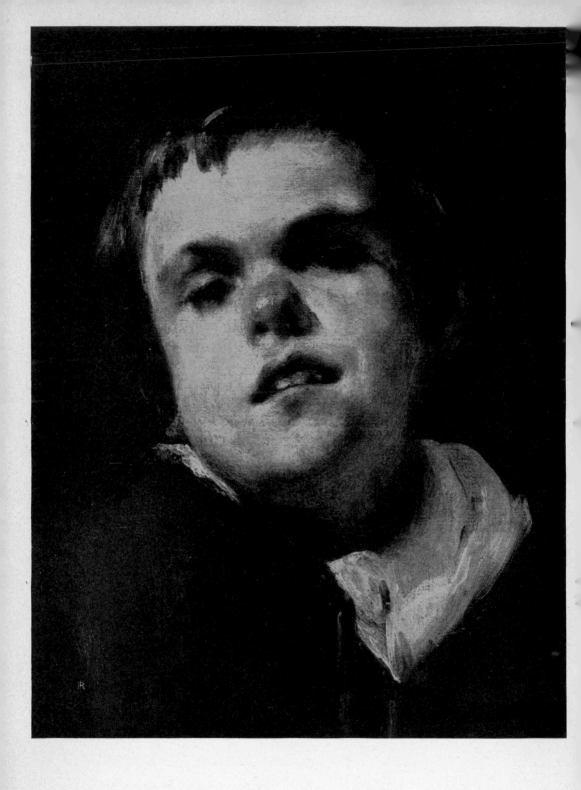

Fig. 25. VELASQUEZ: *The Child of Vallecas* (Detail), c. 1656.

abstraction that he loses sight of his early impression, his work will lack life; it will be a scheme, a symbol, but it will not be art.

Therefore any realistic painting, with any claim to art, puts an accent on reality, embodying it in a style which is the work of the artist's imagination. Some minor Italian artists during the sixteenth century had developed a style called *manneristic,* because it was based on the manner of their masters — Raphael, Michelangelo, or on the Greco-Roman sculpture — instead of on the individual study of nature, and was therefore lacking in the statement of facts. Once when Caravaggio was shown Greek statues for study he made no reply but pointed to a crowd of people to show that nature had provided him with plenty of models. This was his artistic polemic.

Besides, Caravaggio also unleashed a social polemic. His times were dominated by the ideas of the Counter-Reformation, which masked, under a religious cloak, political and social aims. His foes were the advocates of ideal beauty, but they identified ideal beauty with the nobility and the pomp of the upper class.

In spite of his interest in reality, even Titian promoted the grand style mirroring the grandeur of the Spanish "sosiego," as we have already pointed out in Chapter Four. Caravaggio showed in his painting a higher moral standard than his contemporaries and wanted to represent religious scenes through the life of common people. Once, one of his pictures was refused a place on the altar for which it was intended, because it represented St. Matthew in the image of a peasant showing his dirty feet. This will to represent, on an altar, the

99

life of the lowest class of society had a polemical intent directed against the hypocritical self-appraisal of the aristocratic class as being noble and beautiful. For this reason Caravaggio's realism was called vulgar, and ever since all realism has wrongly been called vulgar.

Caravaggio was a Lombard painter (1573–1610), influenced in mannerism by an imitator of Titian. At the time of his birth Titian was still alive and his basic principle of visualizing, like Titian's, was still the effect of light. In spite of that, his style was thoroughly different and new. Figure 20 reproduces his *Call of Saint Matthew*.

In this painting a new relationship appears between figures and space. The prevalence of figures is still as great as in Titian's work. But the importance given to the room where Caravaggio's figures are gathered is more accentuated. The room is present as an element furthering the action of the figures, absorbing them within the action itself. A comparison with *The Sistine Madonna* by Raphael (fig. 11) will show even better the absolute change in the method of visualization.

Similarly, the effect of light is more pronounced in Caravaggio than in Titian. In the room there is an open window, but the most important light illuminating the room does not come through the window but from the right of it, presumably through a window or a door outside the picture. The function of this light is to draw the attention of the spectator to the group of figures seated around the table in the middle of the room. It is for the purpose of telling the story and concealing the rest. If compared with Leonardo (fig. 10), it soon becomes evident that Caravaggio is not making use of universal light, but of a particular light, which has been interpreted by many art critics as night light. No doubt the sharp contrasts between light and shadow suggest night light, with the shadows deep and dark, and the light strong but narrow. But there is no torchlight as in Titian (fig. 18), and the light coming through the window is obviously daylight, however subdued. Caravaggio's light effect is real, but the light is an imaginary one in order to define form more clearly, with its sharp contrasts of light and darkness; it is arbitrary in order to show or conceal what he likes. The legs of Matthew under the table could not be seen so clearly had the light been a natural one. That is, Caravaggio clearly knew that light in painting ought to be an artistic light and not a natural one, and that through the simplification of contrasts between light and darkness, he could achieve a new synthesis of form and expression. This was a great discovery in painting, the discovery of what is commonly known as the luministic style.

Caravaggio's light is useful for telling a story. Christ enters the room from the right alongside the shaft of symbolic light which also illuminates His right hand pointing to the figure of Matthew. Thus light accentuates the significance of Christ's gesture in calling Matthew. Christ is not shown in the foreground; He is seen only through His face and His hand. His presence is thus rendered more mysterious, more of an apparition than of a man. Matthew, seeing the light and understanding the meaning of Christ's presence, shamefacedly points out his fellow gamblers to Christ in order to excuse himself. The other gamblers do not recognize Christ, nor do they understand the meaning of the Stranger's presence in such a place, and therefore do not become part of the dramatic scene, even if they are looking on. Of the five gamblers grouped around the table, the two young, smartly dressed ones appear indifferent to the Stranger's presence. They look at Him but do not understand; while the old man and another young man at the left, who are counting the money, do not seem to be aware of the new significance which the light has conferred upon Matthew. So the character of each personage in this picture is accurately determined and thoroughly revealed, with an insistence which would appear prosaic if compared with Titian's picture (fig. 18).

But it would be erroneous to interpret the light used by Caravaggio as an instrument of psychology only. It is obvious he does not care for beauty but only for the realization of his own vision. The face and the hand of Christ, the hair of the apostle who accompanies Him, the faces, the legs, the hats, and the costumes of the gamblers are excellent achievements, whether considered as powerful color-volumes or subtle nuances of pictorial values.

However, if compared with Titian's (fig. 18), Caravaggio's pictorial values are diminished while his color-volumes are more accentuated. The nuances of light and color, and the representation of movement are much greater in Titian, but the characterization of single images, on the other hand, is much greater in Caravaggio. The sharpness of the contrasts of light and shadow in the latter is used to bring volumes closer to plasticity, and to sacrifice to plasticity color nuances. In Titian, light is so integrated with colors, and so continually in motion with the figures, that the unity of light, colors, figures, and movement is complete. In Caravaggio, instead, there is a contrast whereby the function of light acting against shadow determines static forms even when they are represented in movement. His aim is to present figures poised for action rather than to show the action itself. His painting does not vibrate like that of Titian, and is more a statement of objective fact than a lyrical suggestion. Caravaggio's realism becomes art because it is embodied in a style of light and shade, and because even his individualization of figures obeys an ideal of plasticity. The lyrical unity and the moving lights of Titian produced masterpieces because of the personality of Titian, but when employed by lesser men they could easily fall into a chaos of coloring. A reaction like that of Caravaggio towards more clearly defined volumes approaching plastic form was perhaps inevitable and necessary. It was necessary to limit the vibration of light in order to find a form for volumes, and to distinguish them from the surrounding atmosphere.

In his insistence on volumes, on the external appearance of things, and on material bodies, Caravaggio showed great realism, but at the same time diminished his spiritual power of expression. Through his use of light and shade he founded the *luministic style* — a style of infinite possibilities, but he himself drew only a limited profit from it.

Through his luministic style Caravaggio influenced not only Italian painters but also the best European painters of the seventeenth century, in France and Spain, as well as in Flanders and Holland. But it fell to the genius of a Dutch master to be the greatest representative of the luministic style and to add a touch of magic to his creative power for revealing the human soul. That master was Rembrandt van Ryn (1606–69), whose *The Supper in Emmaus* is reproduced in figure 21.

We have already noted that the use of space around the figure was wider in Caravaggio than in Titian. Space is still more pronounced in Rembrandt than in Caravaggio. This fact has a great importance for Rembrandt as a means of expression. It gives his figures a greater freedom of breath, while his penumbrated nuances on the wall have the function of echoing their emotions. And the height of the wall suggests the monumentality, not of the figures, which are small, but of the event, thus adding to its memorability. There in that poor room, during twilight, something happened which is a miracle.

Entering the room from the left, the light, the source of which is outside the scene, strikes the table in front of the seated figures and then expands around the room. A secondary source of light is Christ Himself, whose head radiates it. However, the most illuminated part of the picture is the cloth on the table. Thus the maximum of light does not coincide with the center of interest which, of course, is Christ Himself. This is due to the use of half-shadows. "Everything is immersed in a bath of shadow, even the light, which later filters through the shadow in order to appear more distant and more radiating. Dark waves embrace the illuminated center, nuancing, penetrating, and thickening them. However, obscurity becomes transparent and half-shadows are easy to perceive. Finally, colors, even the darkest ones, have a kind of permeability which prevents their becoming black." This is a well-known description of Rem-

104

brandt's light by the distinguished French critic Fromentin.[1]

The contrast of light and shade is used by Rembrandt without the sharpness of Caravaggio, while the individual forms are less determined than in Caravaggio and more than in Titian. The center of interest for Rembrandt is not the contrast but the nuances, not the colors but the half-tones. His imagination is given to nuances and through nuances he gives us many of the details of things, but no matter how many details he paints into his pictures their form still remains thoroughly subordinated to nuancing. Thus a nose, a finger, is clearly apparent not in its material form, but as a revelation of a fugitive light. And the light is as fugitive in appearance as the half-tones which suddenly absorb it. The ability of revealing and concealing is unique in Rembrandt. Our experience of a body includes its weight. But the bodies of Rembrandt have no weight. They are appearances revealed through half-shadows. Our experience of emotions excludes their weight. Rembrandt's images represent bodies which seem to be purified of their material consistency in order to become images of emotions. Bodies which are more ethereal than real, lights which are shadows, a cosmic movement of nuancing which envelops even seated figures—this is the essence of Rembrandt's painting. It is an indirect painting. He does not paint what he sees, but what he imagines he sees. Thus he is able to give form to the unseen. But because it is unseen, is it any the less real? Reality is not only seen, but also felt. To "see" feeling, and to reveal it through images is the wonder of Rembrandt.

Once we understand his approach, his artistic coherence for

[1] *Les Maîtres d'Autrefois,* 1877, p. 331.

us is absolute. His effect of light is freer, more imaginative than in Caravaggio. Yet it is more coherent. Recall the legs of Matthew (fig. 20). Caravaggio wanted to show in this picture some well-rounded legs in spite of the fact of their being shown under the table, a place where they would have been immersed in darkness. Rembrandt is not distracted by such formal pleasure. Anything not contributing to his expression is excluded.

With Rembrandt colors are all subdued; yet through their nuances some of them acquire a vibration which is in itself self-expressing.

Plastic form definitely disappears with Rembrandt. A comparison with Raphael (fig. 11) will not only show that a different world was born, but that even Titian (fig. 18) and Caravaggio (fig. 20) have many residues of plastic form. This radical exclusion of plastic form was necessary in order to exhaust the possibilities of the luministic style and reach the painting of emotions.

Another worthwhile comparison would be with Giotto's *Christ* (fig. 2). His emotional power is so strong that it overwhelms the plastic values. He is closer to Rembrandt's Christ than to Piero della Francesca's (fig. 7). Through the most subtle and sensitive medium of light and shade, Rembrandt meets the primitive creation of Giotto, going back to the roots of artistic creation.

Rembrandt's movement is a cosmic vibration of nuanced half-shadows, creating the movement of the figures, but independent of them, because it exists everywhere, even on things which in themselves are static, for example, the wall. Thus the movements of the figures assume a special character. In comparison with Titian, one can readily see that the latter's movements are more pronounced and evident. Rembrandt's movements are restrained, but more intense. Every figure is identified with its movement. Movement reveals its character, its dramatic moment, with a strong accent. Christ is breaking His bread. The two followers dining with Him have different reactions when they recognize Him; one joins hands in adoration; the other shows his astonishment by putting his napkin down on the table. The young waiter sees in Him but a man who ought to eat and does not, and waits. All these emotional and physical attitudes are evident to the very last nuance. But their action comes to an abrupt end. The continuity of their movement is expressed not through their form, as in Titian, but by a tremulous light suffusing the attitude of the various characters. Here we see how movement in a work of art can be expressed independently of natural action and we grasp the importance of the difference between art and nature.

In fact, Rembrandt's whole composition is united by the effect of light — a light bearing no relation whatsoever to geometric form. Through this light the composition of the figures appears even looser than that of Caravaggio. No one so far has succeeded in abstracting a figure from Rembrandt's painting. Rembrandt stresses the whole composition, and the whole is light. If one follows the rhythm of this light he will understand the radiation of light from the table towards the figures. This is the secret of Rembrandt's composition.

The ideal beauty of Raphael is the very opposite of Rembrandt's luministic visualization. The latter is therefore a realist. But a realist of a special kind. Think of Christ, and of all the idealized Christs of the Renaissance. Rembrandt's Christ is "pale, thin, seen facing us, breaking bread as He did on the evening of the Supper, dressed as a pilgrim, with His lips blackened and swollen where torture has left its mark, His sweet, wide brown eyes, largely dilated and lifted to the sky, with His cool halo, a kind of phosphorescence around Him which gives Him an unearthly glory, as one who has without doubt passed through death, yet living. His appearance is that of a divine ghost which cannot be described, the intense ardor of His face, expressed without features, the physiognomy of which is determined by the movement of the lips and the glance — all of this has been inspired we do not know whence, created we do not know how." This again is a passage taken from Fromentin's essay on Rembrandt.[1]

Fromentin was a painter who knew a great deal about drawing and coloring, yet failed to find in this small painting by Rembrandt anything he knew about them. But Fromentin was also a sensitive critic, and became aware of the expression of the soul he had before his eyes. He stated that the expression was realized but he did not know how it was realized. Only by centering our attention on light, on that half-shadow which is Rembrandt's light, on his indirect approach to reality, which transforms a body into a soul, can we understand how Rembrandt achieved his work of art.

For Rembrandt the soul of man was reality. Thus he was a realist — a spiritual realist. And he reached his reality by stripping it of its external material appearance. His painting is unique not only because of his ability to express the soul of man, but also because of his courage in divesting his images

[1]*Loc. cit.,* pp. 356–7.

of any material appeal. His beauty was a purely moral beauty. From an external material point of view his beauty was ugliness. But how then could material ugliness become moral beauty? Here it is necessary to go back from the created painting to the creating man. Sacrifice of material things has always been a way of deepening moral values. Rembrandt's willingness to sacrifice plastic forms, as well as worldly things, such as rich dresses, ornaments, and the pomp of wealth, gave him that humility which is akin to moral life. And he knew perhaps better than any painter before him, after Giotto, the value of humility and self-sacrifice, thus attaining a profound insight into human souls.

But such renewal in the realm of art could not take place without new currents of religious thought. Neither the religion of man of Masaccio and Piero della Francesca, nor the religion of beauty of Raphael, nor Luther's Reformation so bound up with the material interests of German princes, nor the Catholic Counter-Reformation so concerned with worldly power, could inspire Rembrandt's religion. In Holland the Mennonites, a sect seceded from the Anabaptists, had been recognized since 1579. They refused all dogma and stuck to the personal interpretation of the Bible. They refused to take any oath; they refused to be armed and they scrupulously avoided any contact with a sinning world. A moderate, limited, almost unnoted sect, but one of the most spiritual among the sects of the Reformation. This reduction of religion to the individual's moral feeling has been expressed by no one else as well as by Rembrandt. His sacrifice of worldly beauty must have been influenced by the Mennonites' renunciation of worldly life. His renunciation of material appearances in order to reach the depth of the soul seems pervaded by the spirituality of the Mennonites. We have no documents to prove Rembrandt's spiritual kinship with the Mennonites, but his affinity to their conception of moral and religious life exists in his paintings. And this reveals the background of Rembrandt's imagination.

Besides Rembrandt, two other great painters of the seventeenth century, Van Dyck and Velasquez, found in portrait painting their main activity. The frequency and success of portrait painting is a manifestation of the trend of realism.

According to a Greek legend the drawing of a portrait was the earliest work of art. The daughter of Boutades, a potter of Sikyon, "was in love with a youth, and when he was about to leave the country she traced the outline of the shadow which his face cast on the wall by lamplight."[1] Since then portraits in painting and sculpture have been frequent in all epochs and countries, and we may surmise that from portrait-painting was derived the oldest conception of art as an imitation of nature. However, today, and during the past seventy years, it is not in portraits that painting has found its best opportunities. The reason for this is the invention of photography. A star in Hollywood or a political chieftain when dedicating his or her image to a crowd of admirers prefers to deliver his photograph. Every artist or art lover will protest that the photographer will never render the intimate character of the sitter, as the painter can and often does. And this is perfectly true. But the intimate character of the sitter is due to the interpretation of the artist, filtered through a personality for-

[1]Pliny's *Natural History*, XXXV, 151.

eign to that of the sitter. The artistic value of a picture of a tree depends on the personality of the painter and not on the tree. Likewise, the artistic value of a portrait depends on the personality of the painter and not on that of the sitter. The interpretation of the character of the sitter may be successful, but it is always a subjective interpretation, and when the objectivity of it is insisted upon too much the work of art loses its value. Furthermore, the sitter changes not only with age, but also in different states of mind. Thus what is called the intimate character of the sitter is only the fugitive impression the painter received from the sitter when he was looking at him. This fact is responsible for the lack of resemblance among different portraits of the same person. Different photographs of the same person resemble each other much more.

Thus if one wants to understand the artistic value of a portrait, he must look at it as a painting, and not as a portrait; as a painting like any other painting.

However, one must admit that portrait painters were helped by their own genre to avoid ideal beauty. It is difficult to find ideal beauty embodied in a single person, and even women interest painters more for their characteristics than for their beauty. Portrait painting stresses the characteristics of the sitter, which always impresses a certain intensity of life on the work of art. Nature being always irregular, the irregularities in the features of the sitter helped painters to abandon their ordered conventions and to find a relation between them and reality. This explains why in the past so many portraits were masterpieces. But today the old scope for recording the features of a person no longer prevails, photography having been entrusted with it, nor are the ordered conventions still alive in the best of our painters. Thus, portrait painting has lost much of its importance in recent years. Photography has seen to that.

Figure 24 reproduces the *Portrait of a Cardinal* by Raphael. The Cardinal, no doubt, belonged to a very aristocratic family. Nevertheless, we may be sure that the ideal of Raphael in painting this portrait was to identify his ideal of formal beauty with the nobility of the sitter. Probably because of the selected circle he lived with, Raphael was the first to apply to the highest social class his nobility of form. The refinement of the features of the sitter, the simplicity of his appearance, the detachment and aloofness of the image, and the predominant cardinal red against the dark wall, all these elements concur in the expression of beautiful and delicate nobility.

Obviously Raphael did not care to register his personal impressions. There is neither a hint of Raphael's first impression of the Cardinal, nor any knowledge of his life and deeds. He would still remain anonymous even if we knew his name. This portrait represents a type of social function and a social class, and it represents, too, the cultural and sophisticated life of a very high civilization.

Figure 23 represents the *Portrait of Jacopo da Strada* by Titian. We know that the sitter was a painter from Mantua who was interested in antiques and later became an antiquarian, collecting antiques for the Emperor Rudolf II. But even if we did not know this, we should still be aware that the sitter is a rich and dignified man, handsomely dressed and interested in antiques, since he is here portrayed with a statuette of Venus in his hands, and also a number of old coins.

Baudelaire said that a portrait can be poetry or history. Of course if it is purely history, it is not a work of art. However, one may see a great deal of difference between these two portraits, one by Raphael and one by Titian, the former's being purely lyrical poetry, and the latter's containing in his poetry many elements of history.

As has already been pointed out, Titian's style aimed at the immersion of human figures in the surrounding atmosphere. It was not only a visual but a moral immersion. A man does not live in a moral void; he acts, he moves towards somebody or something during every moment of his life. Titian profited by the freedom of movement effected by his use of light and shade and succeeded in portraying his model not as an abstract type but as a living being. Even better, he succeeded in portraying him at that particular moment which suggested the character of his life.

Raphael begins with his ideal beauty and through the generalities of a class and a civilization reaches the individual sitter. Titian begins with his fugitive impression of an individual moment and through the generalities of a class and a civilization reaches the universal value of life. In both portraits there is a coincidence of ideal and reality. But reality being Titian's aim, the ideal element is within his imaginative reality. There is no longer an ideal impressed on reality, or, better, an ideal so pronounced as Raphael's ideal of beauty. Titian's reality creates its own ideal by its own power, its ideal consisting in its participation in universal life. Thus the historical and the poetic values of Titian's portrait coincide.

Rembrandt painted numerous portraits of himself, with an interest in the individual moment, in the fugitive impression, more intense than Titian's. In portraits of other people Rembrandt knew how to express the characters of his models. But when he painted himself, even his character and his resemblance were outside of his interest. His self-portraits bear little resemblance to one another. As for beauty, he was not an Adonis and he knew it very well. Perhaps this was the reason why he preferred himself as a model. What he cared for in portraying himself was the effect of light, and to vary it he often dressed in bizarre costumes. Figure 22 reproduces a portrait of himself holding his palette. His image, dark against a light background, with the light on the rag and on the face clearer than on the background, results in a magic effect where reality appears with a strength unknown to nature. This is a pictorial reality parallel to but distinct from the reality of nature. And in this distinction lies the artistic value of his painting.

The luministic style requires physical ugliness, to show its best effect. This principle is apparent even in Velasquez (1599–1660), the Spanish painter who as a man was as distant from Rembrandt as he could well be. He was concerned with the physical aspect of things; and his art consisted in the emphasis on color-volumes, on their solidity, their evidence, and their living substance. As a young man he liked to portray the popular life of the taverns (*bodegones*). But after 1623, at the age of twenty-four, he became portrait painter to the King of Spain and his court, and succeeded in giving the required emphatic nobility to his portraits. And sometimes he indulged in portraying beautiful models, always with an unsurpassed objectivity. His power of realization was beyond any limitation. His work seems impersonal and it does not reveal what he felt or dreamed.

However, at the court of the King of Spain lived certain buffoons and freaks. Velasquez portrayed them, and even outside the court he found certain idiots suitable as models. Here we must emphasize that these buffoons, freaks, and idiots suggested to Velasquez, because of their deformities, some of his masterpieces. *The Child of Vallecas,* whose face is reproduced in figure 25, is one of them. The vividness of the light causes the idiot's smile to vibrate in a powerful way, beyond his physical appearance. The evocation of life is so intense, the luministic style so coherent in its destruction of form, that the artistic value appears absolute. This image has a magic power depending solely on the effect of light. Hence the similarity with Rembrandt's portrait of himself.

Neither Giotto, Masaccio, Pollaiuolo, Titian, nor El Greco aimed at beauty in their painting. Yet theirs are among the recognized masterpieces of mankind. But Rembrandt and even Velasquez sought ugliness through which to achieve their masterpieces. Realism was a condition of this negation of beauty. But above all it was the effect of light, absorbing the attention of the greatest painters of the seventeenth century, which enabled them to perceive the human soul through ugliness and to let it vibrate freely.

Chapter Six

ART AND ILLUSTRATION

Fig. 26. GOYA. The Execution of the Third of May
Fig. 27. MILLET. The Angelus
Fig. 28. MEISSONIER. 1814
Fig. 29. COURBET. The Stone-Breakers
Fig. 30. TOULOUSE–LAUTREC. A la Mie

BEFORE printing was invented in the fifteenth century, manuscripts of poetry, history, and religion were illustrated with miniature paintings and drawings done by hand. After printing was invented, engravings on wood or metal were substituted for miniatures. The purpose of both was to comment on the text. The text of the book furnished the illustrator with the subject matter to which he dedicated his creative imagination. However, even if the imagination of the illustrator enjoyed a certain creative freedom, its scope was always bound to be restricted by its faithfulness to the text. Thus the limitations of the illustrator, as an artist, parallel those of the portrait painter obliged to reproduce in his painting a certain likeness of the sitter, which is also an artistic limitation. With the illustrator it is a moral limitation; with the portrait painter it is a physical limitation. The illustrator is the portraitist of an event; the portrait painter, of a living person. However, it is important not to confuse

Fig. 26. GOYA: *The Execution of the Third of May*, painted in 1814.

Fig. 27. MILLET: *The Angelus*, 1859.

Fig. 28. MEISSONIER: *1814*, painted in 1864.

ig. 29. COURBET: *Stone-Breakers*, 1849.

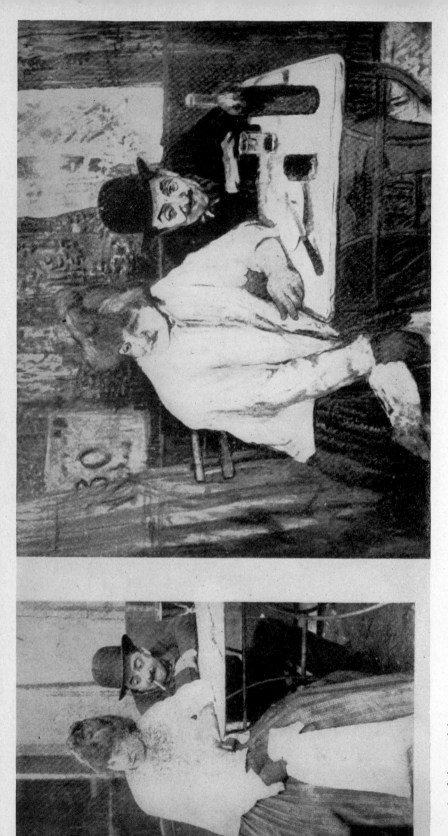

Photograph of the models.

Fig. 30. TOULOUSE-LAUTREC: *À la Mie*, 1891.

an illustration with a real work of art. You cannot, for example, consider Piero della Francesca's *Resurrection* an illustration. It is true that it represents an event in the Gospels, but the imagination of the artist goes so far beyond the mere historical fact that the *Resurrection of Christ* is no longer an illustration of the religious event recorded by the Gospel, but an event created by Piero della Francesca. Thus interpreted and transformed, the illustration of an historical event or material fact ceases to be a mere illustration and becomes a form of the artist's imagination, that is, absolute art.

Since the beginning of the nineteenth century, when the interpretation of all human events became subject to the historical approach, history has assumed an importance unknown before that time in human culture. This historical interest has become so widespread as now to encompass all phases of human activities from heroic deeds to the minutiæ of everyday life. Therefore it was quite natural that painting too should come under the influence of this historical approach, and that events, important or not, should appeal more than ever before to the artist's attention. The painting of history — that is, of historical events — became fashionable and more accurate in portraying historical details than heretofore. And since illustration is the portraiture of events, every painting of history has been illustrative in character. Only rarely, when the imaginative genius went beyond the representation of the historical event and transformed it into a new independent pictorial event, did the absolute work of art appear.

It can be said that realism in the seventeenth century was chiefly concerned with portrait painting. But in the nineteenth century a new kind of realism made its appearance, that is, the portraiture of events, or illustration.

Francisco Goya (1746–1828), a Spanish painter, managed to embody in his paintings a new content with such compelling interest and authority that he influenced the best art of the whole nineteenth century. Perhaps the masterpiece of Goya is *The Execution of the Third of May* (fig. 26). It represents the bloody repression of Spanish patriots defending their soil, by the French soldiers of Napoleon I on May 3, 1808. This picture shows a group of men terrified and desperate, in the act of being shot by the French soldiers, while another group of people are shoved forward to the spot where they too are to be executed. It is Hell—and only on a distant height, a village representing the indifference of nature to human events is visible to offset this human tragedy. Goya painted this scene in a diagonal composition in order to accentuate through the space occupied by his figures the certainty of the event. The form of the composition is revealed by light or suggested by shade in such a way as to give it a square-shaped, sketchy, dynamic character, and a spirit as positive as it is violent. The light is concentrated on a man in shirt-sleeves, opening and raising his arms, betraying by his gesture the tragedy of approaching death.

To understand this painting it would be helpful to compare it with *The Supper in Emmaus* by Rembrandt (fig. 21), taking into consideration the many changes in thought and social life that had occurred in the meantime. Rembrandt's scheme is a religious one, with an intensification of the expression of a spiritual life unknown since the religious fervor of the Middle Ages, thus renouncing all physical beauty in order to lay bare the beauty of man's soul. And in order to give a universal character to the spiritual life of his personages he chose, as prototypes for his painting, men and women belonging to the common herd of humanity and not to the upper classes of society. Since Raphael, the identification of ideal beauty with the nobility of a social class had been the rule. The contempt heaped on Caravaggio's realism as being vulgar was due to social prejudice. Rembrandt was, of course, entirely free from this prejudice; his religious feeling, idealizing his images of the common people, gave them a moral beauty. This idealization transcended reality.

The new contribution of Goya to art was the abolition of all transcendency in painting. This does not mean that Goya lacked religious feeling. As a man he adhered to the faith and practice of Catholicism, even though he was conscious of the vulgarity, hypocrisy, materialism, and corruption of the clergy of his day. And in his *Caprichos* he freely expressed his rebellion against them. But the content of *The Execution of the Third of May* does not include Catholicism. The feeling responsible for it was his intense love of liberty and country, and he rebelled against the cruelty of the mass execution of his people by foreign soldiers. The lazzarone[1] who opens his arms in this tragic scene is the new Christ once more on Golgotha. The historical significance of this epoch-making painting is this: by stressing the motif of a new religion of freedom, liberty, and humanity, ushered in by the French Revolution, Goya also expresses his own personal religious convictions.

[1] A name applied, in Spain and in Italy, to beggars, harmless loafers and tramps.

Looking at *The Execution of the Third of May,* no one can possibly think that the soldiers who are doing the killing are doing their duty, or that the beggars are in themselves the heroes of Spanish freedom. The only possible interpretation of this painting is that a blind machine is crushing a human value, assuming epic proportions purely and solely because of this contrast between a human value and the inhumanity of a machine. Goya here represents the revolt of popular passions, and sanctifies them. He suffers and cries out. Thus his powerful visual expression goes beyond the tragedy of the third of May and the patriotism of Spaniards — it assumes a universal human value. Goya's picture is an eternal symbol of the popular revolt against cruel oppression.

This new content has its new form giving rise to a new conception of *finish* in painting. From Raphael through Titian to Rembrandt there is a gradual detachment from the finish. The effect of light and shade does not allow the painter to heighten the contours and components of a figure as plastic form does. The subordination of all elements in a painting, either to the accents of light, or to concealment by shadows, limits the finish. A difference results between the finishing of an expression and the finishing of the things represented. For example, Rembrandt still preferred to finish accurately some of the objects shown in *The Supper in Emmaus,* as the dishes and the knife on the table show. But Goya rigorously limits the finish to his dramatic effect.

This new conception of finish influenced Goya in his indifference to ideal beauty. Any seeking after plastic beauty would have destroyed his expression. Imagine a beggar at the point of death assuming a theatrical pose in order to appear a hero! The absurdity would destroy the tragedy of the event. Goya's imagination is here at work on a reality which antecedes any distinction between beauty and ugliness. If he had made such a distinction the figures isolated from the ensemble would appear like caricatures. But in the ensemble they appear tragic, intensifying the effect.

In order to understand how this can happen it is well to recall the origin of caricature. At its origin, caricature was not connected with the comic. Forms of caricature were created in order to depict the character of things with simple straightforwardness. Beauty required a selection of some elements of nature and the exclusion of others in order to find an artistic reality parallel to, but distinct from, naturalistic reality. The ideal of characterization, too, was a selection and an exclusion, but following principles totally different from those underlying beauty. Characterization accentuated the elements which could express the sublime, the comic, the tragic. Goya emphasized the characterization of violent contrasts, of the dismay in nature, of the animality in man, thus creating a form where the comic and the tragic coexist without any distinction whatsoever between them, and through them he realizes monsters of intense humanity. This is the reason why *The Execution of the Third of May* goes far beyond the historical event, tragic as that may be, and attains a new artistic form through the universal value of art.

Here it is necessary to stop a moment in order to ponder the relationship between the story in *The Execution of the Third of May* and its form as we have tried to define form. And it may also be well to point out here that the story is only a pretext, a good pretext indeed, to fire Goya's passion for patriotism and revolt—but only a pretext. The content of this work of art is not the event which took place on May 3, 1808, but Goya's passion for patriotism and revolt. It was this passion that conditioned Goya's artistic form and brought the artist to the exploding point of his expression. There are thus three factors to be considered in this picture: the historical event, the artist's feeling, and his form. The historical event is an objective fact, but feeling and form are subjective qualities partaking of the personality of the artist. Only subjective elements—feeling and form—are essential to the work of art; the event is contingent.

What must be avoided in the appreciation of a work of art is to base one's judgment on the story, on the object, or on the elements which are not directly connected with the subjectivity of the artist. But here a problem arises. There are paintings which reduce the story to a minimum, even to nothing; and other paintings, on the contrary, which insist on the representation of the story. Is there a yardstick with which to measure the artistic value of a painting? Which is better, a painting which tells a story or a painting which does not? Personally, we do not think there is such a measure of judgment. The artist is free to find his inspiration wherever he likes, and to express his feeling and create his form as he pleases. But the condition governing the realization of a work of art is that the story, if any, be used as a pretext and not as the content of his work. The event of May 3, 1808, aroused Goya's passion, and it is this passion which gave form to his masterpiece. But think of other painters who have a story to tell and wish to tell it as accurately as they can, and, considering the representation of it their most im-

122

portant aim, relegate their form and feeling to a secondary, subordinate position. They can succeed in so doing, and often are successful in their effort, but their work will have a practical social value rather than an artistic one.

Look at the works of Giotto, Piero della Francesca, Raphael, Michelangelo, and Titian: their ideal of form, plastic or pictorial as the case may be, is evidently predominant over the interest of the subject matter. But what can be said of Rembrandt? Certainly the story is, for example, more important for Rembrandt than for Piero della Francesca. But in Rembrandt the effect of light, the nuance of shadows, the proportion of figures and space, reveal the subjective feeling of the artist with such an emphasis that the story is thoroughly subordinated to it. The same can be said of Goya. However, the fact that the representation of a story is more important for Rembrandt and Goya than for Piero della Francesca or Raphael has its place in forming a critical judgment of them. The following statements will clarify this point.

Piero della Francesca and Raphael surface-finished their paintings more than Rembrandt and Goya did. Their indifference to the story permitted them to give their pictures a more thorough finish. The purpose of this finish was the presentation of bodies and not the representation of stories. But when the representation of stories became important, the painter had to run the risk of sacrificing the finish of his forms: otherwise these could become the forms of the story itself, but not of his imagination. This was the only way to translate the story in terms of the creative artist. And this is the intimate reason for the birth and development of the luministic style in modern art. This style was a defense of the creative artist against becoming the slave of the subject matter, since the more the subject matter became contemporaneous, the more urgent the danger became. Christ in Emmaus was a subject already mediated by tradition and often treated in art. But the Execution of the Third of May was a pressing contemporary event and therefore much more urgent to the soul of Goya. Thus Goya's painting was not as finished as Rembrandt's.

This dramatic urgency expressed in a loose finish was not understood by many painters of the nineteenth century, and since their paramount interest was the story the artistic value of their paintings was weakened. Thus criticism considers them illustrative painters, that is, belonging to an inferior level of art. Of course an illustrator can also be a first-class artist, when he goes beyond the limitations imposed on him by the subject matter and conceives a form which has a character of its own. But if his work is motivated solely by the subject matter, then he is an illustrative painter — a painter who cares more for the practical purpose of entertaining the public than for expressing his most intimate and individual personality.

Jean François Millet (1814–75) was for a long period of his life ignored, then suddenly glorified with perhaps more adulation than any other painter in the nineteenth century, and then once again almost completely forgotten. Now a new effort to revive his fame is being made. Contempt and enthusiasm for him as an artist depended mainly on the subjects of his paintings. Van Gogh adored him, copied some of his figures, but painted them in a thoroughly different manner. Today the tentative revival of his paintings coincides with the preaching of a return to the subject matter. It is true that Millet created some stories in painting which are as moving and unforgettable as the story of a popular novel. He had a flair for drawing and his drawings were competent and accurate. His coloring is conventional and poor, but generally not offensive. And the sentiment he felt for the peasants he represented was sincere, since he knew them intimately, for he himself came of peasant stock and often lived among them. Finally, he had a genuine religious feeling, social sympathy and generosity, and a deep feeling for poetry, which he somehow managed to communicate to us through his pictures.

All of these are the elements for a great art. But was he a great artist? Perhaps the most famous of his paintings is *The Angelus* (fig. 27), which shows two peasants, man and wife, bowed in prayer, listening to the tolling of the angelus bell from the distant village church as the day's work is done. This scene is enacted in the foreground of a broad, flat, expansive field while the light is still strong in the sky, but subdued on earth. The seriousness of their religious piety is emphasized by the solitude of the land and the wideness of the horizon. Millet wrote to a friend: "When I was painting *The Angelus* I remembered when I myself worked in the fields. When the angelus bell rang my grandmother made us stop working and with our heads bowed and bared we recited very piously the ave for our departed dead." Thus the remembrance of his personal experience added a touch of intimacy to the expression of the painting. Yet in spite of all this pious sentiment Millet's painting fails to convince us as a work of art. The sympathy Millet felt for his fellow peasants spurred him to come to their defense before the Parisian public in behalf of their piety, purity, and cleanliness. He saw them as poetic subjects, and refined them in order to convince the French people of their proletarian rights. In this, he was morally and socially right, but his painting was the painted speech of an able lawyer. The work of the artist is something different. Even worse, he faked his beloved peasants in order to make them more acceptable. If one wants to be aware of the eternal verity of a peasant, he must look at the *Card Players* by Cézanne (fig. 41) and not at *The Angelus* by Millet. Millet's scene is sentimental. A painting to be art must have feeling. But genuine feeling is a living approach to reality while sentimentality is a will to convince through sentiment, and a mistake in taste. And a will to sentiment destroys natural feeling.

One of the essential qualities required of an artist is sincerity in his work. And Millet no doubt was perfectly sincere in his beliefs. But there is a certain misunderstanding about sincerity in art. One can be sincere in his theoretical manifesto if he believes in it, but to be sincere is not enough for transforming a theoretical manifesto into a work of art. One can be sincere in his moral action, like Millet, but he cannot expect his action to be considered a work of art even if realized through painting. Mere sincerity of thought, and the will to do, do not necessarily constitute art. When we ask for sincerity in art what we really mean is *spontaneity*. In fact, the process of feeling and imagination which goes on in the artistic process must not be interfered with by conflicting interests, intellectual or moral, even if they be sincere. The artistic process must be as natural, that is, as spontaneous, as the growth of a tree, or the flowering of a blossom. Spontaneity is, of course, always sincere, but it is also something more.

Millet's drawing fared no better than his composition: it is competent, accurate, and sure; but it is not creative drawing. It is self-conscious, acquired, conventional. Millet had learned the academic way of drawing and never thought of revolting against the learned conventions; he preferred to use his drawing as a means of propaganda. It was noble, honest, human propaganda. But propaganda is never art, nor is drawing merely a means, in the hands of an artist. Drawing is an art in itself, and when used as a means to an end, it ceases to be art. Art is lacking when a convention is not transformed into an individual creation.

His coloring is even more conventional than his drawing, accentuating, as it does, with its nuances, the sentimentality of the ensemble. Even on moral grounds one may object to *The Angelus*. Fake peasants and conventional sentiment, skilful drawing and coloring, do not produce honesty in art. And as for its educational value, only dupes can be convinced; intelligent people never will be.

However, *The Angelus,* being a typical example of centering the attention on the subject matter instead of on the sensible form, has its importance. The excessive finish of the silhouettes of the two peasants robbed Millet of the effect of light — that revealing-concealing approach to painting, which, if used properly, would have impressed on his characters the individual imagination of the artist. Likewise he refined his peasants and his form too much, taking them out of their class. The acceptance of this painting by the well-to-do classes, who approved of such respectful peasants, explains the reason for its success. But all this has a value only within the limits of practical social activity. It is not enough for an artist to invent a nice subject and show ability in representing it. It is necessary for the artist to go beyond his subject matter, and reach the realm of free imagination transforming the elements of nature or an intellectual thesis into creative art. It was the thesis which he belabored that steered Millet's sentiment onto the wrong road and made him lose his natural talent in conventionality.

Gustave Courbet (1819–77) was a much finer artist than Millet. They were contemporaries; both wanted to preach the proletarian credo, both were champions of realism. But Millet considered himself a poet and a religious man and did not find the connection between his religious poetry and his form; hence his unconscious hypocrisy. Courbet, on the contrary, proclaimed himself an enemy of the ideal, of the poetic and of the religious; he had of course his own ideal, but it was the opposite of what his contemporaries considered the ideal. Against ideal beauty, against choice in nature, with a thorough faith in the pictorial power for reproducing physical things as one sees them, against the upper classes of society, because of their snobbishness and pretension to culture, Courbet stuck to the earthiness of the people and their ways of life. Thus his ideal and his motives were in perfect accord. If his tendency to preach and to impose his credo through his painting, brought him too, like Millet, to rhetoric, one must admit that his power of realization and his enthusiasm for achievement pushed him, many times, beyond rhetoric into the realm of art. And this was due to his natural feeling for form and coloring. His form was academic, and often it is nothing more than a display of virtuosity. Sometimes, however, this virtuosity led him towards freedom of creation, and then his form, in spite of its academic origin, became art. His feeling for coloring was deeply sensual, but he abstained from intense color, finding in its subdued tints a unity which was a constant nuance of diffused light. This light effect was aided by the thickness of the tints which Courbet obtained by substituting the palette-knife for the brush. The readiness and skill of his hands made it possible for him to treat the dense material of his hue with a lightness of touch as though he were using the thinnest of brushes. And so he realized the transparency of light in half-tones not by delicate brushing but by the coherence of his thick touches. That is, he obtained the synthesis of the light of each color rather than the mixture of the color substances themselves. And it is this synthesis which gives the most material of his color-volumes wings of poetry.

On November 20, 1849, Courbet wrote to a friend: "I was riding along in my carriage on my way to the château of Saint-Denis, close to Maizières. I stopped along the road to look at two men breaking stones. It is rare to encounter a more complete expression of misery." He invited the two poor devils to his studio and painted *The Stone-Breakers* (fig. 29). In describing his painting, Courbet wrote: "All this takes place in the broad sunlight, beside the ditch of a highroad. These men stand out against the green slope of a great mountain which fills the canvas and over which are projected the shadows of the clouds; only in the right-hand corner the slope of the mountain allows a little blue sky to be seen. I invented nothing, dear friend; every day when I went for a ride I saw these men. Besides, in such a state, that is how you end."[1]

It is well to recall that a year before Courbet painted *The Stone-Breakers* the great revolution of 1848 had taken place, which suggested to Karl Marx the Communist Manifesto. This was the moral atmosphere in which Courbet breathed. Thus in his painting there is human sympathy, and feeling for the disinherited. But a political thesis is not apparent. However, contemporaries realized that Courbet "had revived the social question without wanting to by merely pointing out injustices."

As for the art in his work, the critical problem consists in determining whether, and where, the universal feeling of human sympathy is expressed at the expense of furthering the social question. In other terms, it is necessary to understand whether the individual misery of *The Stone-Breakers* is related to the historical revolution of 1848, in order to be used as a political pamphlet, or whether it heightened the level of a universal and eternal human sympathy, which is the level of art.

To answer this problem it is well to recall the explanation of Goya's unfinished form. Courbet's form is much more finished than Goya's. He wants to prove, to demonstrate, the misery of *The Stone-Breakers:* thus the tattered shirts, pants, and vest of the figures. This insistence was due to Courbet's desire to show his virtuosity, but his virtuosity was put at the

[1]G. Riat, *G. Courbet,* Paris, 1936, p. 73, and *L'Amour de l'Art,* October, 1935, p. 385.

service of a rhetorical display of misery. Moreover, the attitude of the younger man in the picture is as objective as a photographic image, and the details of the tools on the ground have the same objectivity, distracting the observer from the unity of the scene. But the figure of the old man has a thoroughly different character. It shows no action, his hard work is presented in a perfectly balanced attitude, that is, the natural representation of the old worker has been substituted by an ideal presentation of an old sufferer. Every element of his body is related to a surface that by its pattern and volume reveals the meaning of the image. This figure of the old man is static, totally lacking in action, precisely in order to stress its volume, a volume which is given life by the effect of light and shade. This formal synthesis of pattern and volume has such vigor that the result is one of monumentality. Here the human sympathy of Courbet found its own form, becoming the symbol of the sympathy felt for the misery of all old workers. If, after having felt this sympathy for the image of the old man and having realized its artistic value, one studies the image of the younger man in the picture, one soon becomes aware that the latter does not express anything, bears no relation to the old one, and is the work of a good artisan in painting, rather than that of an artist. Courbet's virtuosity sought after an ideal sphere of art, sometimes reaching it, but more often than not falling back on the satisfaction of denying that very ideal, or of furthering social action. His realism brought him great renown; but if his art still lives today, he owes it to the few rare free images he painted, such as that of the old stone-breaker.

If Millet's *Angelus* is a work with many artistic elements

gone astray in the labyrinth of a religious-social rhetoric, Courbet's *Stone-Breakers* has many elements foreign to art, but in one image of it he reached the level of great art.

Ernest Meissonier (1815–91) painted many military scenes, such as *1814* (fig. 28), depicting Napoleon's French campaign, and enjoyed a great popular success among his contemporaries in spite of the contempt felt for him by true artists. Compare Meissonier's Napoleon and Courbet's stone-breaker, and there is no doubt which of the two men is the hero — the hero is the stone-breaker. Napoleon is reduced by Meissonier to a puppet for children. Manet said that Meissonier painted everything in iron but the armor. Meissonier boasted of his knowledge of the structure of horses, but the white horse mounted by Napoleon is a dead animal without either structure or movement. He dreamed of representing heroic events of French history, but succeeded only in reducing every hero to the kind of puppet found in genre scenes. The greatest ability he had was to show minutely finished details, the while losing sight of the whole. The reproduction of one of his works here has no other purpose than to show how disgracefully the method of thorough finishing was followed in the nineteenth century; for the more precisely the details in a picture are rendered, the lower falls the level of the picture as a whole, until even photography would despise it.

Another ability displayed by Meissonier in this painting is that of having caught the resemblance of Napoleon and his marshals. They can easily be recognized, and no doubt satisfy the curiosity of people. Curiosity is the only appeal of Meissonier's paintings. But the pleasure of recognizing, on the streets of New York, some king or queen or princess on a shopping tour, is a pleasure which bears no relation to what one should feel in looking at a painting. Still another penchant of Meissonier was that of painting everything belonging to the high life of the upper classes of society — a stone painted by Courbet is proletarian, but the snow painted by Meissonier is aristocratic, thus unwittingly adding an accent of absurdity to the heroic pretensions of the painter. Millet was at least sincere, even if not spontaneous in his painting, but Meissonier was sincere neither towards his theme, his vision, nor his feeling. He was sincere only in his ability to repeat with an incredible precision what he had learned in his academic training. When one cannot feel music he is said to be deaf; in this sense, certainly Meissonier was blind.

If Meissonier was blind, Henri de Toulouse-Lautrec (1864–1901) was a seer. He belonged to that tradition of illustrators who had for their spiritual fathers Goya and Daumier. His posters were not only the best ones done at the end of the nineteenth century, but by their originality they also influenced the best posters of our century. The special type of illustration which is proper to posters, with its sharp impact on the spectator's imagination, is evident also in Toulouse-Lautrec's paintings.

Figure 30 shows, at the right, a painting of a man and a woman sitting at a table, by Toulouse-Lautrec, entitled *A la Mie, mie* in French being a familiar, confidential name for a woman. At the left, it shows the photograph taken of the same two figures at the time they were posing for the painter. The man, Maurice Guibert, was a friend of the painter; the woman was a pretty professional model and both were quite innocent of any evil implications in their pose. But Toulouse-Lautrec wanted to represent a scene from the seamy side of Parisian life, its apaches and prostitutes. Thus he deformed the pretty young woman into an old worn-out, miserable slattern, and the gentle friend into a degraded ruffian. The portrayal of such misery is striking and therefore the illustrative quality of the painting is very high. But what can we say of its artistic quality? Think of composition. The photograph shows the composition to be unbalanced. Lautrec advanced the figure of the man in order to correct the diagonal composition by a hint of its development on the surface. He added a bottle of wine in order to compensate for the body at the left with something at the right. He gave a false perspective to the plane of the table in order to give it reality, and a basis to the whole group. The figures in the photograph are isolated from the wall. Lautrec found a relationship between the figures and the wall by depicting the wall with the same variety of brush strokes with which he painted the figures, thus achieving an expressive unity of both figures and background. In the photograph, the room is just a room; in the painting the room is a tavern, as vicious as its inhabitants. The impact of such expression on us is not therefore through our association with some specific experience of reality, but through the powerful effect of its brush strokes, that is, directly through pictorial means.

Lautrec's transformation of his friend into an apache is a caricature, and not a happy one; he insists too much on this deformation, with all humanity lost in the result and with only a mask of the man remaining. Here we see the case of an artist too close to his subject and not detached enough to be able to see his image as a living creature. The face of the apache is no longer the face of an individual, but of a type. It has become a pictorial scheme with which to display the apache type, and since all schemes are abstractions this is a dead face without artistic life. On the contrary, the woman, however repugnant, is full of life. Notice how conventional is the appearance of the woman in the photograph. In the painting her hair becomes a pictorial wonder, her left hand revealing in its vulgarity her whole life, and her attitude and look having the compelling power of bringing to the surface her obvious intentions, her natural baseness and habitual drunkenness, with a portentous evidence.

Thus this illustration of the apache world is a partial masterpiece in painting, with a mistake in the figure of the man preventing it from being a complete one.

Henri de Toulouse-Lautrec came from one of the noblest families of old France, and was destined for a life of indolence and ease like his father and relatives. But when a boy he had his legs broken twice and developed a physical deformity which made an outcast of him. The contrast between the very high social position of his family and that in which he found himself, because of his disability, was reflected in his character. As an outcast he became bitter; and, in self-protection against his wounded feelings, flaunted all social conventions of behavior and traditional respectability. Deeply stung by the hypocrisy of his society, he fought against it with the cruelty of his drawing. But this forced separation from his birthright grieved him so deeply that he did not laugh lightly at examples of vice and degradation, but depicted them instead with a cruel evidence of social responsibility and pervaded by a grief which in reality amounted to genuine sympathy. His figures of vice became the mirror of his desperate life.

As often happens to artists of the temperament and infirmities of a Lautrec, his life was too closely bound up with his art. He was not sufficiently detached from the reality of his subject matter always to create a work of art. Hence his shortcomings, as in the figure of the man where the effort of deformation was too pronounced, prevented his imagination from remaining on the level of art. On the other hand, the transformations of the pretty model into an old prostitute, and of the plain room into a vicious tavern, were the result of a free imagination, removed far enough from all his resentments to become translated into lines and colors, thus acquiring artistic quality. One can say that the figure of the woman fully attained its artistic form, form understood not as objective form, not as form in general, but as the individual form of Toulouse-Lautrec. A general form for prostitution would be an illustrative form. But the individual form of Toulouse-Lautrec is indeed a purely artistic form.

Chapter Seven

VITALIZING NATURE

THE GREAT majority of the paintings studied so far have been compositions of figures each telling a story. From them we have also learned that for a painting to be considered a work of art it had to meet certain conditions, namely, that the story had to be absorbed and transformed into an ideal motif and artistic form, showing the artist's power of visualization and feeling. Of course, since ancient times artists have been conscious that it was their form and not the story which gave artistic value to their paintings. But æsthetic thought was slow in growing, hence the necessity of telling a story in a painting in order to hold the spectator's attention. The "historic genre" in painting — that is, paintings with a story to tell or an historical event to illustrate — was considered even during the nineteenth century the most noble, important, and successful genre in painting. A landscape without human figures in it was considered a secondary genre. This conviction was predicated on the assumption that

137

man, as an image of God, and his deeds were the most praise-
worthy subjects to be represented. This is the reason why, for
a long time, landscape was conceived only as a background
for human figures, such as we saw in the paintings of Giotto
(fig. 1), Piero della Francesca (fig. 7), or of Titian (fig. 16).

It is true, as we have pointed out, that the pictorial form
was the result of a vision where the human figure was no
longer isolated from its surroundings, but immersed in the
atmosphere it breathed. That is, elements of the world, such
as trees, mountains, and sky, attracted the artist's attention no
less than human figures, and influenced by their presence the
form of human figures. This was a conception of reality,
embracing the entire world, enlarged beyond the scope of
man, and reducing man to a simple element of the universe.

However, before the nineteenth century, landscape painting was only one of the many genres represented in the art
of painting that had some indirect influence on the general
development of taste, though this happened only occasionally in the long history of the art. On the other hand,
during the nineteenth century it was landscape painting
that became the leading factor in taste. This means that in
the nineteenth century landscape painting was something
entirely different from a genre. It became an ideal — the essential ideal in painting that found in landscape its best way
to artistic expression. Of course individual artists, when favored by genius, had always been able to paint landscapes
which were perfect works of art. But only during the nineteenth century did the exceptional achievement of a few individuals become the general trend among creative artists.
This was the effect of a new conception of landscape as a

138

Fig. 31. CONSTABLE: *The Hay-Wain* (Creation), 1821.

Fig. 32. CONSTABLE: *The Hay-Wain* (Replica), 1821.

Fig. 33. COROT: *The Bridge at Narni*, 1826.

Fig. 34. MONET: *Sailboat at Argenteuil*, 1875.

Fig. 35. PISSARRO: *Oise River near Pontoise*, 1873.

"state of mind," that is, of the complete humanization of nature.

Before the nineteenth century the principal trends of landscape painting may be summarized as follows:

Giorgione's *Thunderstorm* (fig. 15), as already noted in Chapter Four, was a landscape lyrical in character and based on the spontaneous discovery of nature as a means of expressing human sentiments. However different in style, the landscapes of Titian and Peter Brueghel, for instance, also belong to this same category.

Later, in the seventeenth century, some Italian painters began a new genre in landscape painting, brought to its highest realization by a French painter, Nicholas Poussin. This was the historical genre. It was peopled with human figures representing certain heroic deeds, and its purpose was to tell a story or to illustrate an historical event. It used nature as a means for amplifying the story, for giving it a cosmic echo. Thus it sometimes realized qualities of monumentality and grandeur that had previously been rendered only in figures of human beings.

During this same period still another kind of landscape painting made its appearance in Holland, having as its chief characteristic a portrait-like quality, of which Jacob Ruysdael and Hobbema were the leading exponents. As all things have the weakness of their strength, the weakness of this landscape painting was too often its accurate topographical character, without sufficient feeling in its expression for the things represented. Nevertheless, this naturalistic accuracy often served, when feeling and imagination were really working together as in Ruysdael and Hobbema, to transform the things in nature into a personal style, thus giving birth to some very well-known masterpieces.

Following this naturalistic trend, it was not until the eighteenth century, especially in England, that a new kind of landscape painting called *picturesque* made its appearance. The picturesque was defined by Price[1] in 1794, as having roughness, irregularity, continuous variation of forms, colors, lights, and shade. It was a reaction against the monumentality associated with the sublime. These two contrasting views found their concrete manifestations in the casualness of the English garden as opposed to the formal Italian-French architectural garden, the former allowing nature to dominate with its spontaneity, disorder, and surprise. By the same token, a natural view was appreciated, not so much for its structural formation, balance, and order, but for its unexpected variety and irregularity.

This idea of the picturesque had a great influence on the landscape painting of the nineteenth century, but it also had certain limitations not always favorable to the realization of art. In fact, it must be pointed out that before the picturesque made its appearance, there was the pictorial — the picturesque being a projection in nature of a mode of seeing and feeling — which had been inaugurated by the Venetian painters of the sixteenth century, and developed through the Baroque period of the seventeenth and eighteenth centuries.

And, as already noted in Chapter Four, the pictorial is a form not based on drawing but on the relationship of colors. Titian's form, for example, is a pictorial form, and a perfect artistic form because all its components are perfectly coherent.

[1]C. Hussey, *The Picturesque*, London, 1927, p. 66.

But this coherence cannot be found in nature, which has always something of the chaotic, and the picturesque found in nature can never present that coherence which is proper to the pictorial form. Thus the picturesque, in spite of its having opened our eyes to artistic suggestions previously unnoticed in nature, can never, of itself, result in a real work of art.

These were the conditions governing taste at the beginning of the nineteenth century, when a new impetus was given to landscape painting by the convergence of various artistic trends.

Jean Jacques Rousseau (1712–78), the Geneva philosopher, had advanced man's confidence in and reliance on nature, as an escape from the artificialities and frustrations of modern civilization. For many centuries the place offering sanctuary from worldly trials and tribulations had been the church, the house of God. Rousseau suggested that the human urge for the divine could be found in nature. This was pantheism — an echo of Bruno's philosophy of a cosmic God immanent in all created things, animate and inanimate, in the universe — from the smallest particle of matter to the sun and stars, from the lowliest living thing to man. In its relation to painting this new conception meant that nature was regarded as a living entity and was approached with a sort of religious devotion.

John Ruskin (1819–1900), the English writer, described this change of mind in relation to nature in the following way: The ancient Greek cast nature entirely "into a human form, and gave his faith to nothing but the image of his own humanity. What sympathy and fellowship he had, were always for the spirit *in* the stream, not for the stream; always for the dryad *in* the wood, not for the wood. Content with this human sympathy, he approached the actual waves and woody fibers with no sympathy at all." We Christians, "imagining our God upon a cloudy throne, far above the earth, and not in the flowers or waters, approach those visible things with a theory that they are dead; governed by physical laws, and so forth. But coming to them, we find the theory fails; that they are not dead; that, say what we choose about them, the instinctive sense of their being alive is too strong for us; and in scorn of all physical law, the wilful fountain sings, and the kindly flowers rejoice. And then, puzzled, and yet happy; pleased, and yet ashamed of being so; accepting sympathy from nature, which we do not believe it gives, and giving sympathy to nature, which we do not believe it receives, . . . we fall necessarily into the curious web of hesitating sentiment, pathetic fallacy, and wandering fancy, which form a great part of our modern view of nature."[1]

Of course, such a "pathetic fallacy" concerned thinkers, rather than painters who were ready to believe in the spiritual life of trees, rivers, and mountains. Theirs was love, enthusiasm, and rejoicing for a sunny landscape, and theirs a deep sympathy for the humble and shadowy aspects of nature. To see how such enthusiasm and sympathy took artistic form one has but to look at certain living landscapes painted by genuine creative artists, both before and after Ruskin.

John Constable (1776–1837), the English painter, was the earliest artist to impart this new feeling for nature to his landscape paintings. His ideas on this score are as impressive

[1]Ruskin, *Modern Painters,* Part IV, Chapter XIII, § 13.

as the quality of his works. He wrote: "The landscape painter must walk in the fields with an humble mind. No arrogant man was ever permitted to see nature in all her beauty." And again: "I never saw an ugly thing in my life: for let the form of an object be what it may — light, shade, and perspective will always make it beautiful."[1]

Constable's humility was necessary to him in order to approach nature with true devotion, and to leave him free to look at nature in his own way, which for him was the artistic way. He loved nature, all of nature, without prejudice and without preference. By him everything in nature was considered beautiful, not because everything is beautiful in itself; in fact, nothing being ugly in itself, nothing can be beautiful in itself. Everything in nature can be made to appear beautiful, that is, everything can be made beautiful by art. It is art which masters light and shade, and perspective. And it is light and shade which give form to Constable's art. He does not portray trees, water, and sky as such; but instead he creates light, shade, and distances.

Thus shorn of subject matter, Constable goes on from there to find the coincidence of form and content in his own creative imagination. In fact, light is his passion, the religious mood of his vision. He says: "Everything seems full of blossom of some kind, and at every step I take, and on whatever object I turn my eyes, that sublime expression of the Scriptures — 'I am the resurrection and the life' — seems as if uttered near me."

Constable thoroughly understood the uniqueness of any

[1]C. R. Leslie, *Memory of the Life of John Constable,* London, 1937, pp. 367, 406. The passages following: *loc. cit.,* pp. 103, 368.

143

work of art, each one having its own law, right for itself and wrong for all other works. He says: "Every truly original picture is a separate study, and governed by laws of its own; so that what is right in one, would often be entirely wrong if transferred to another." This detachment from the things represented obliged him to stress his own mood and mode of visualizing.

There was a belief in art criticism prevalent for a long time that a painting in order to be considered finished had to reproduce the objective likeness of things in nature. To obey this tradition meant for Constable to subordinate his content to the subject matter, thus lessening the artistic quality of the painting. It meant, further, to introduce into his artistic creation some element from the outside, such as the rules imposed by the Royal Academy and accepted by the public, or a thing imposed by nature, a tree or a house, without first transforming it into a unified vision. Thus, forced by the material circumstances of his life, Constable came to a crossroads. He had either to bow to the dictates of the Academy and public opinion or to be faithful to his own feeling and vision. He chose both ways: in his best period, when his style was thoroughly matured, he painted various pairs of landscapes. One was painted in accordance with his own ideal to please himself, and the other to meet the requirements of the Academy. He considered the first as finished as soon as he had caught his feeling of light and shadow and his vision of space without in the least bothering about the delineation of things in nature as such. It was a finished picture, finished insofar as his own personal expression was concerned, but not insofar as the representation of things would have required.

It has often been called a sketch — a *creation* would be more appropriate and accurate. And because he was aware that his contemporaries would not appreciate his creations, he kept them to himself. And he sent the other painting of the pair to the exhibitions of the Academy, this *replica* being finished in accordance with the demands of the Academy and the public; that is, finished insofar as the naturalistic representation of things required.

A comparison of the two components of the pair — the creation and the replica — is instructive in order better to understand Constable, the artist, and Constable, the man, and to distinguish the artistic personality of the one from the practical personality of the other. Figures 31 and 32 reproduce the pair, called *Hay Wain,* painted in 1821. In his creation, the artist takes possession of space; space is represented pictorially, and not according to scientific perspective as in the replica. In the creation, every image is alive with light — light being the essential element in his painting unifying his style. Light reveals or conceals, gives life or takes it away, pausing to caress or ready to flee, insofar as it has captured the painter's heart and insofar as he is more or less moved by it. The replica, on the other hand, represents the things of nature in themselves and, in addition, the effect of light on them, with the result of attracting the observer's attention in two different directions which never coincide. The one is the empiric or prosaic vision of an object, figure, or scene, of the world; the other is the poetic interpretation of light. In the prose work all is finished, in a fixed way that partakes of death, and all the particulars in their objectivity reflect a general indifference.

145

For instance, look at the roof. In the creation, it is a mass of colors revealed through subdued lights, partaking of the universe and giving a sense of the infinite. In the replica, it is a series of colored tiles with each tile neatly set off by itself and finished like the work of an artisan. And the same can be said of the water or of the human figures.

The colors, which in the creation are the very material of which the light is made, are in the replica an unnecessary veneer of a form existing by and in itself. The distant meadow is yellow — a dead tint in the "finished" picture, and a precious light in the "sketch." In the creation, the silvery reflections of the clouds in the water freely intermingle with the brown reflections of the shadowy earth. In the replica, the water is a gradation of a substance of monotonous gray-green, without the real quality or texture of a liquid. In the sky of the replica there are windless and stormless clouds, paper clouds, but in the creation the sky announces a veritable storm, justifying the contrasts of light and shade on earth, and causing the ancient trees and the house and the water to pulsate with life. There is no uncertainty here, but a genuine emotional vitality within the unity of a vision resolved in a chromatic contrast.

Every stroke in the creation expresses the artist's sympathy with and joy in nature; in the replica we have, on the contrary, the bare demonstration of a material reality. Poetry and prose, love and indifference, the infinite and the finite, knowledge of the imagination and knowledge of the intellect, rarely are they opposed to one another with such clearness as in these two pictures.

In his replicas, Constable showed the ability of the technician, of a realist, minute, diligent, tenacious, of the earth earthy, and he showed, too, his preoccupation with worldly success, which, however limited, allowed him to live. But when he painted to please himself in accordance with his ideals of art, as in his creations, his concern was wholly with light, shade, and space, with his enthusiasm for nature, and with his feeling for the rural aspect of the English country-side he loved so much. There he transformed everything under the sky into a unified artistic vision. There he belonged to the absolute realm of art, and not to worldly contingencies. There he was the pure artist.

Camille Corot (1796–1875) was a thoroughly different man from Constable; besides, he was a Frenchman, and belonged to a later generation, as one may readily see by noting the dates of their death rather than those of their birth. Corot died thirty-eight years after Constable.

But the troublesome problem of "finish" was the same for both, and Corot, like Constable, solved it in the same way — by keeping for himself the original creations finished to the point of perfect expression, and by sending to the Paris Salons the replicas finished in accordance with public taste. This happened, for instance, when in 1827 Corot sent a replica of *The Bridge at Narni* from Rome to the Salon in Paris (now in the National Gallery of Ottawa), accurately painted but devoid of any life. It was a replica of an original creation inspired by the actual bridge (fig. 33). The yellow of the bare earth and the green of the plants and the grass are very low in tone. Near by, the river Nera is turbid and sandy until, through the shadow of the bridge in the middle distance, ap-

147

pears the clear blue of the water flanked by the gray-greens of the hills and the blues of the shadows, until in the far distance appear the blue mountains veiled in mist under the pale blue of a sky broken by white clouds. With a few intense blacks the painter plunged right into the battle of light and shade over the broken ground and the ruined bridge, a battle which finally spends itself in the distant azure of the sky. From the neighboring tumult of life to the distant, yearned-for peace, this is the theme of the picture.

The pictorial process has been explained by Corot himself in this fashion: "In preparing a study or a picture it has seemed to me very wise to begin by indicating the most vigorous values (supposing that the canvas is white) and to continue by following in the right order up to the highest values. I should begin by setting up 20 numbers, from the most vigorous dark tone to the highest light tone. In this way your study or picture would be set up in the proper order. This order should in no wise trouble the draughtsman or the colorist. Always the mass, the whole, that which has struck us first. Never lose the impression that has moved us first."[1]

As is well known, Corot has not always adhered to his maxims. In fact, the contrasts of light and shade will often give way in his paintings to an unopposed domination of half-tones and nuances. But whatever was lost in robustness and energy was gained in delicacy and grace. The sunlight of Rome gave him the energy of contrasts; and this energy remained with him as the necessary antidote to a slackness which always lurked as a constant threat behind the artist's simplicity and good nature.

[1] E. Moreau-Nélaton, *Corot raconté par lui-même*, 1924, Vol. I, p. 126.

148

An important consequence of this mass-vision of dark and light tones is the avoidance of a natural foreground. By drawing into the foreground of the picture a distant point of the landscape, Corot interprets rather than reproduces nature, and himself partakes in the life impressed on things by lights and shadows rather than materially reproducing the details of things, and thus achieves the transmutation of things into life-values. Since the value is the infinite and the object is the finite, in order to rediscover the infinite in the finite the artist requires detachment from his object, a vision just as distant materially as it is near spiritually. He does not lead the spectator by the hand to a view of nature in depth, but presents to him an object seen on the surface, in which there is something near and something far, but seen as a whole detached from the observer. Both the near and the far belong to the world of the infinite, the world of art, distinguished from the world of nature. This is why a little rough earth and turbid water, a broken bridge and a few distant hills, have become an absolute of art, a wonder of the world.

This need for an effect of distance in the foreground of the picture necessitated the "unfinished" quality of the painting as a consequence of it. If we reflect on the way the idea of finish was interpreted in his day it was but natural for Corot to feel every image becoming material, step by step, as it was being finished. Hence the uncertainty and even the awkwardness in the execution of his paintings, for each time it seemed as though he wanted to finish them according to the unwise advice of others. His timidity did not permit him to rebel openly against this finish quality, he merely contented himself with evading it. Although lacking in theoretical consciousness, there was fortunately in Corot an overbearing will to go his own way. He himself remarked how in Rome he once freed himself of the advice of his teacher Bertin. "I came to the decision never again to return home without work done at a stretch, and attempted for the first time a drawing by mass, a rapid drawing, the only kind possible." Baudelaire, the French poet, was practically the only one who as early as 1845 denied Corot's "awkwardness," who distinguished the *finished* from the *created,* and who affirmed that a work of genius is always sufficiently executed.

Here it is necessary to indicate briefly the major trends of taste to which this painting is related. In 1827, when it was painted, there were two contrasted schools of painting: the neo-classical and the romantic. Corot had been educated in the neo-classical school; that is, in the school where the tradition of historical landscape painting, and of Poussin, prevailed. The romantic school was revolutionary and its aim was to stress sentiment and passion, heroism and drama. Corot, in the replica of *The Bridge at Narni* sent to the Salon, followed the neo-classical principles, but not in his creation reproduced in figure 33. However, his rebellion had very little to do with the romantic principles. True, like the romanticists he visualized nature as contrasts of light and shade, and infused that contrast with dramatic power. But the calm, the construction, the lack of emphasis in the whole painting have no romantic character. On the other hand, he did not allow his imagination to wander beyond reality, but sought his imaginary creation within the limits of reality, of the natural reality he saw. Thus he was a realist, but one who refused to paint the detailed objectivities cherished by the realists.

150

Refusing detail, he stuck to his impression of light and shade, and no sooner had he realized this impression than he stopped. The thrill of perceiving the struggle of light and shade in the foreground, and his ecstasy for the clarity of the horizon, became completely fused in and absorbed by his visual impression.

Corot made a choice, not from among the things of nature, but from among the elements of his mental process. He did not want to apply any established rule; he did not want to preach any ideal, moral or otherwise; he wanted to be faithful to his impression. The naïveté of his character permitted him to see nature as no one before him had seen it, and his modesty and good nature permitted him to be content with the realization of his vision within the limits of his impression. Nor was he aware that by this re-creation of a primitive vision and by this accepted limitation of adhering to impression, he had fathered a revolution in painting which went far beyond the romantic revolution, and even beyond the Realism created twenty years later. He even went so far as to anticipate Impressionism, which was ushered in more than forty years later. Impressionists invented a technique very different from Corot's, but the visualizing of *The Bridge at Narni* is impressionistic. Neo-classicism, romanticism, realism, impressionism are trends of taste. In each one, real artists created works of art, but no trend in itself was ever directly responsible for the creation of art. Therefore it cannot be maintained that *The Bridge at Narni* is a work of art because it anticipated Impressionism. Yet this anticipation was the proper way for Corot's genius to reveal itself, and for the intimate freedom of his imagination to be realized. Thus it is this anticipation which permits us to see in the personality of Corot his power and his grandeur as an artist.

Impressionism as a trend in taste is illustrated by figures 34 and 35. It was realized by a few painters in Paris, between 1870 and 1880. It broke sharply away from the Western tradition of painting and its influence was exceptionally widespread. It is still alive as an element in taste today. It modified not only painting, but sculpture, literature, music, and criticism as well. In spite of some of Renoir's figure compositions, the easiest and most usual realization, as well as the historical origin of Impressionism, was in landscape painting.

In the years just prior to 1870, three young men, Monet, Renoir, and Pissarro, used to sit on the banks of the Seine and the Oise rivers and paint landscapes. They were realistic painters, greatly interested in rendering the reflection of light on the water, which showed continuous movement and gave a new life to the water. Furthermore, the various colors thus reflected suggested to them the idea of expressing light by opposing colors without using dark tones for shadows. And so they clarified their palette unconsciously, and divided colors, not by following any theory, but only by experience. For some time, they painted water in this new way, and hills, trees, houses, and sky in the old realistic traditional way. However, this resulted in unbalanced canvases. To avoid this mistake, they then tried to portray everything, even human figures, in the same way that they painted water. They saw every image not in abstract form, not in chiaroscuro, but as a reflection of light, either real or imaginary. They had selected only one element from reality—light—to interpret all of nature.

But then, light ceased to be an element of reality. It had become a principle of style, and Impressionism was born.

Light is the element which reveals the appearance of reality. What Impressionists painted and interpreted was not reality but the appearance of reality. They stuck to the appearance of things with a clearer vision than had painters before them. The grasping of appearance is a form of sensation, sensation as free from reasoning and will as it can possibly be. Thus Impressionists were faithful to their sensations, that is to their impressions of nature, and found a form closer to the first impression of the appearance of nature than previous painters. And it was closer because of their vivid sensibility, whereby they understood the absolute value in art of the appearance of things, nor did they undervalue their impressions since their mind was sufficiently free from the traditional principles of abstract form.

The first step in art is the contact with the appearance of nature. It is the essential condition in art without which there can be no art. Raphael or Rembrandt, for example, realized the appearance of things. Then, through their imaginative process, they went farther in order to reach a physical or moral ideal which was beyond sensation. The Impressionists found their physical and moral ideal within the limits of their sensations. They forsook many possible developments of their imagination in order to make sure that the sensible actuality should be perfectly realized.

Impressionism was a reaction against Realism, against the objectivity of Realism, and an emphasis on the rights of subjectivity, of the personality of the artist, in his creation of art. This detachment from objectivity was an ideal, but it was

153

not an intellectual ideal because it was based on sensation.

Impressionism was also a reaction against Romanticism, a revolt against human passions and their manifestations in poetical, historical, or political guise. Thus the subordination of subject matter to motif, as we have already noted in Giorgione, became a normal habit of the Impressionists. And they also disregarded all illustrative material of contemporary life, because by adhering to the properties of water, trees, skies, or of the common man, they represented a life which is eternal as well as contemporary.

Impressionists painted simple trees instead of monumental ones; peasant cottages instead of palaces; plain girls instead of great ladies; workingmen instead of noblemen. This was not for the purpose of advancing a political issue, but was the expression of a natural sympathy towards familiar subjects, familiar to their everyday life, the life of poor people and open country. In the old historical landscapes an oak is always a nobleman; an impressionistic poplar is just a common man. This meant the discovery of a new source for art.

We saw how Constable and Corot were able to break down the tradition of formal finish in painting, but we also know that they didn't dare exhibit their creations and instead made finished replicas in order to bow to public opinion. But Impressionists showed a better consciousness of their art and exhibited their creations, stopped painting when expression was fully realized in their canvas, without concern for the approval of the public. Thus it was Impressionism which imposed on public taste a finish which is associated only with the expression of the artist, and not with the accurate representation of things and their details.

154

The composition of Impressionist painters was a composition of light, and not of things represented. The arrangement of things in balance, or the representation of space in perspective was lacking in their paintings. Hence they were accused of painting only fragments. This is rather amusing. Where is the painter who can represent the whole of nature? Every artist, of course, represents mere fragments. True, painters concentrate on each fragmentary element their feeling for the whole of nature, which is nature itself. So did the Impressionists. They had selected light as one of the many elements of nature. They had endowed their own created light with their artistic quality, and had subordinated all other elements to their light. One can be aware of the totality of their works of art, only if he sees the expression of their composition of light.

The most evident, and the most recognized, quality of the Impressionists was that their paintings were brighter than all other paintings since the sixteenth century. This was due above all to the division of colors we spoke of. The bright effect of this division of colors was due to the fact that the fusion of two lights is brighter than the mixture of the two corresponding tints. If, for example, you mix two tints, one blue and the other yellow, you obtain a green with some quantity of gray which lessens the intensity of the original blue and yellow. But if you juxtapose the blue and the yellow, at a certain distance the eye sees a green, resulting from the lights of the blue and the yellow; and this resulting green will be much more intense than if you had mixed the two tints. Impressionists never followed a systematic use of this fusion of lights, but they reached this result through their sense of coloring, the most subtle the history of art has ever known.

This division of colors required an appropriate form. Plastic form in painting was appropriate to chiaroscuro, as in the works of Raphael. On the other hand, Titian, Rembrandt, and, in the nineteenth century, Goya, for example, had realized a pictorial form, different from the plastic one, because it mainly depended on the general effect of the tonality of colors. But when colors were divided, the painter was compelled to modify form to a greater extent than when colors were not divided. In the original of figure 34 the purple roof of an orange house is reflected in the water: the reflection is a series of tremulous zones of yellow representing light, and of purple representing shade. This division of two colors emphasizes the vibration of the reflection. But through that division the form of the roof is lost; what remains is the form of the vibration. And correctly so; for had the form of the roof been maintained the vibration of the reflection would have disappeared, and the purpose of the painter would have failed. This is the reason why so many painters who adopted impressionistic colors but remained faithful to traditional drawing and to chiaroscuro, lost both form and color. Thus the division of colors is at the very basis of that distortion of form which is typical of modern art and which for many different reasons has been adopted by so many painters, even by those who refused to use any division of colors. Impressionists, for the first time, conceived a distortion of traditional form, as the necessary form for divided colors. Of course, they realized it much more easily in the image of a sky, a river, a sailboat, or a tree, than in the human figure, as we shall see later in these pages. This is one of the reasons why Impressionism originated with landscape painting, and was only later applied to human figures.

When the division of colors was adopted, the conception of space had also to be changed. Florentines in the fifteenth century discovered perspective and used space as a void wherein to isolate human figures. With Leonardo and the Venetians of the sixteenth century, aerial perspective was added to linear perspective in order to represent not empty space but a space full of atmosphere. And as the atmosphere was deepened through the effect of color, a three-dimensional effect, full of nuances, less sharp and better related to the surface, was finally realized. Now consider the atmosphere of a picture suggested by the vibrations of divided colors and full of light reflections, and you will soon realize the necessity for the painter to diminish the three-dimensional effect in his painting. The fact that in an impressionistic painting the painted surface prevails over the illusion of space in depth has been one of the charges made against the Impressionists — an unjust accusation because there is no law which requires of a picture a three-dimensional effect, and the Impressionists in emphasizing the surface of their paintings were perfectly coherent in their use of light through divided colors as the unifying factor of their painting.

Finally, the conception of movement held by the Impressionists was also an entirely new one. As their painting had its origin in the reflections of light in water, the whole effect of their pictures was due to a perennial movement, a cosmic vibration. Any static object introduced into that vibration, would have destroyed the whole effect of their art. To visual-

157

ize a cosmic vibration meant for them to reveal the impression of that energy which is the life of nature. Vibrating light was for them the force which endowed everything in nature with life and vigor.

Thus the Impressionists brought pictorial form — that is, the form of color — to extreme consequences, undreamed of before them. In later years, some Impressionist painters fell prey to a certain vagueness of coloring without proper form, thus resulting in foggy effects which were unconvincing. But this was a failure evident in certain works by a few later painters only, not a failure of the Impressionists during their heroic period between 1870 and 1880, and it is not found in the paintings reproduced in figures 34 and 35.

Figure 34 reproduces *Sailboat at Argenteuil* by Claude Monet (1840–1926), painted in 1875 during the best period of his activity. Both the sky and the water in the picture are dominated by the action of the sunset, with the orange, yellow, and purple tones vibrating with the pagan abandonment of an orgiastic festivity, and yet, withal, somehow calmed by the green and blue into a perfect balance. The sailboat, slightly off center in the picture, done in opaque almost neutral green, is the pivot around which light dances; while in the sky the sun, in its last daily salute to earth, spreads its gem-like treasure of light, and reflects it into the water. But with the suggested calm of the evening approaching, the opacity of the sailboat suggests the lull after the orgy. The excitement with which Monet painted this picture is evident in his divided colors and in his clarified palette, as well as in his furious brush strokes. The painter here seems immersed both in the movement of colors and in the vibration of light. His enthusiasm here is at its height, the wonder of nature completely overpowering him. And yet he is not joyous in this profusion of nature's bounty. He feels the coming end of it all, and it is precisely this pervasive sentiment of melancholy which results both in the balance of colors and the human expression of nature.

The personal accent of Monet is on the wonder of nature, but he balanced it by the variations of his color nuances, so that it might become natural. And since his aspiration was always towards the wonder of nature he invented the impressionistic touches, not only for dividing colors, but also to express directly through them the vibration of nature. This was an innovation in painting as daring as it could possibly be, and was no doubt prompted by an inner necessity to rebel against traditional modes of expression and by a faith in his own mode of expression unequalled among his fellow Impressionists. It was indeed Monet who started the offensive for "plein air" in painting — that is, painting directly out of doors from the motif, without in the least caring for the finish of the studio. And because of this he was recognized as the leader of Impressionism. This, however, does not mean that Monet was the greatest artist among Impressionists, but that he was the leader of that revolution in taste. The greatest artists are perhaps less daring than Monet was; they are less exclusive; they usually fashion their style with a more comprehensive mind, and they seldom stress the unusual wonders of nature. In later years Monet, more and more convinced that in art the vibration of light was all, lost even the hint of visual images and of space, painting some foggy

159

mixture, where even light disappeared altogether. This later production of his is in itself the most severe criticism that can be levelled against him as an artist, where the will to succeed and to impose his point of view in art undermined that earlier source of spontaneity and inspiration which is the glory of the *Sailboat at Argenteuil*.

Figure 35 represents the *Oise River Near Pontoise* by Camille Pissarro (1830–1903), painted in 1873. In this picture the flowering earth, the water, the factory buildings, the sky — every bit of this canvas — vibrate with the light Pissarro painted in it. But this vibration is not the only subject matter of the painting, as in Monet's. There is also a very well-defined construction of space in depth from the right foreground to the left middle ground. However, Pissarro does not lose sight of the surface by the emphasis put on the horizon and the ample sky above it. His free touches of light are impressionistic, as is the form of the flowers, of the reflections of light in the water, of the buildings, and of the clouds, in the picture; it is always the form of the effect of light, and not of the things in themselves. This emphasis on the effect of light is more evident in the flowers than in other passages of the picture, because they are in the foreground. But it none the less motivates all other aspects of the painting as well. And in accordance with the impressionistic principles of seeing things, the colors too are as bright and intense as the light. But the contrast between light and shade in Pissarro's painting is more pronounced than in Monet's, so that the form acquires a greater volume, a greater stability, in perfect coherence with the composition. This stability, however, does not lessen the vibration and the vitality of anything in nature; but the vibration is slower and larger, and is thoroughly integrated with the construction of the picture.

Pissarro's eye is less excited and his contemplation of nature is calmer, even if the vibration gives the vision a hint of drama, sufficient for vitalizing nature, but mastered by a deep sense of reality. Pissarro did not seek wonders in nature. He believed that *all* of nature was wonderful and that the most wonderful of all wonders was the everyday life of nature. He is at the same time more, yet less, of a realist than Monet. Pissarro sought to retain in his pictures the freshness of his first impression of nature, but always worked accurately to transform it into a unity of pictorial effect, so that he eventually became more detached from nature than was Monet. Such an attitude was responsible for the accurate construction of his paintings, the volume of his masses of colors, and finally for the preciousness of color itself, which in his best works is unsurpassed.

He has often been accused of being prosaic, and his subject matters are indeed prosaic. But Pissarro's poetry exists, even if it is necessary to find it, not in his subject matter, but in his form, his light, and his colors. No painter so far has surpassed him in his feeling for nature and in endowing it with life. Nature for him was a matter of faith, a moral principle. He believed that the society of his time was corrupt — an evil to be avoided — and found his right to freedom and humanity only in contact with nature. This moral attitude made it possible for him to impress his landscapes with his utter faith in the life of nature.

Chapter Eight

MODERN PHYSICAL BEAUTY

Fig. 36. TOULOUSE-LAUTREC. The Woman Clown Cha-U-Kao
Fig. 37. BOUGUEREAU. Nymphs and Satyr
Fig. 38. RENOIR. The Bather
Fig. 39. VAN GOGH. The Arlesienne

THE *Nymphs and Satyr* by Bouguereau (1825–1905) (fig. 37) was painted in 1873 at the very beginning of the Impressionist movement and is a perfect example of that academic conception of form which was destroyed by Impressionism. The aim of Bouguereau was to realize a classical beauty. Of this painting Frank Crowninshield wrote as late as 1943 that "The Nymphs were conceived a good deal as the classical poets — Ovid, let us say — would have imagined them, though a little immaterialized by reason of their white and pearl-like lustre." Now, please look at the classical conception of form by Raphael (fig. 11), and by Ingres (fig. 12), and you will soon realize that Bouguereau's form has the distinctive character of a lie, without any serious effort to portray beauty. The aim of this kind of beauty is pleasantness, but in this picture not even pleasantness is achieved, because to be pleasing a thing must be alive. And these forms are dead. They are naked models reproduced through learned schemes of form, without any sensitive feeling for naked beauty. They are abstractions devoid of

162

Fig. 36. TOULOUSE-LAUTREC: *The Woman Clown Cha-U-Kao*, 1895.

Fig. 37. BOUGUEREAU: *Nymphs and Satyr*, 1873.

Fig. 38. RENOIR: *The Bather*, 1874-75.

Fig. 39. VAN GOGH: *The Arlesienne*, 1888.

any feeling for reality, of any artistic ideal. The feeling for reality would have determined the individual form of the models, but Bouguereau avoided this in order to show that he knew how to correct reality for the purpose of attaining an ideal beauty. On the other hand, an artistic ideal of beauty would have stressed the presentation of beautiful forms; and this Bouguereau avoided in order to tell a story, the story of how certain nude women enjoyed themselves trying to force a resistant satyr to take a bath. And to illustrate this story he suggestively painted the curved back, the enticing breasts, and the rounded arms of the women. He prostituted himself, together with ideal beauty, in order to please people who lacked both ideal values and healthy sensuality.

In spite of all this, which is quite evident, the painting has been recently praised because the "bodies, faces, hands and feet are a miracle of draughtsmanship and modeling." Please look again at the Madonnas of Raphael and Ingres and notice how solidly built they are even though resting on clouds. Bouguereau's nymphs are not placed on earth at all, and are thus totally lacking in any plastic quality, which demands that an object be firmly set in a given place. One may try to defend Bouguereau by saying that he wanted to represent his figures in movement; but we have only to look at Titian's *Christ Crowned with Thorns* (fig. 18) in order to realize what movement in painting is, and to understand that Bouguereau's nymphs are totally lacking in any movement and instead assume poses which, being unbalanced, pretend to imitate movement. Besides, there is no sense of space at all in the picture, and the landscape around the figures is merely a badly painted back-drop fit only for a third-rate show. No doubt, Bouguereau in this canvas thought he was portraying ideal beauty, plastic qualities, movement, and space, but what he actually offered were mere artificial substitutes. Why? Because his purpose in portraying beauty was vitiated by the necessity for a meretricious attractiveness; because the plastic qualities were vitiated by a specious refinement of the bodies; because the movement was vitiated by the desire to show only suggestive parts of the bodies; and because space was destroyed by stressing the figures. These contradictions reveal that the result is a lie.

Adolphe Bouguereau, a professor at the Académie des Beaux-Arts from 1876 on, had a distinguished career as an academician. In his teaching as well as in his work he always repeated what he had learned from his confrères and predecessors in the academy, spreading painted lies which were taken for truths, in order to please a public devoid of any consciousness of art. By his lying, he shows that he lacked moral consciousness, and by repeating conventional forms, he shows that he lacked artistic consciousness, which is consciousness of the creative character of art.

There would have been no need to speak of him or to reproduce any of his works had not a recent exhibition of the *Nymphs and Satyr* in New York attained a shameful public success, which shows how disorientated is the artistic taste of today. Furthermore, this picture shows how decadent was the academic taste in Paris in the 'seventies, at the very dawn of a new era in painting, and reveals the necessity for a militant attitude on the part of creative artists to combat this kind of academic and critical influence and to maintain the standards of real beauty in art.

164

The Bather by Renoir (1841–1919) (fig. 38) was painted a year or two later than the *Nymphs and Satyr* by Bouguereau. Renoir's painting is a great work of art, a work of real beauty, but a beauty created from new sources — from the feeling and imagination of the artist and not from conventionalities tiresomely repeated. At a glance one can readily see that Renoir's nude is full of life, that it is realistic, that the painter does not conceal a single wrinkle of the skin in its right place, and that it is at once both an ideal of the monumentality of the body and of its radiant appearance. No doubt this is one of the most glorious achievements of Renoir in his early Impressionistic period, and it is an achievement of beauty. However, if we take Raphael's *Madonna* (fig. 11) as the prototype of classic beauty, we ought to admit that Renoir's beauty is not classic at all.

The reasons for the different kinds of beauty as between the works of Raphael and those of Renoir are infinite. But two reasons will suffice to make clear the distinction between them: one is the different tradition of visualization, and the other the different ideals held by the two painters.

In order to understand Renoir's form it is necessary to remember that from the Venetian painting of the sixteenth century on, form was conceived not as closed and isolated from the surrounding atmosphere but as open and immersed in the atmosphere. Thus form was rendered not through the modeling of chiaroscuro, but by the effect of light and shade on the object painted. This conception of form had been developed through the subsequent centuries and had become a common ground for the best painters from the seventeenth to the nineteenth centuries. In the latter century this conception was enhanced by landscape painting. Constable said that he had not seen an ugly thing all his life, because whatever be the form of an object, "light, shade and perspective will always make it beautiful." This was the credo of many good painters in the nineteenth century, and it was Renoir's credo, too. His sense of beauty was not that of the object itself but of light and shade. In *The Bather* of Renoir, Constable's principle of landscape beauty has become a principle of feminine beauty. Thus both the figure and the setting participate in the action of light and shade in this picture, and there is no longer a figure isolated from its background, but both figure and background form a unique effect. The beauty of the picture is due to this effect, and not to the human image itself.

Raphael's ideal of beauty, following his own idea of it, was the result of a selection from among the elements of nature in order to recompose them into an organic whole. Renoir's ideal of beauty was also a choice, but not from among the elements of nature; it was a choice from among the elements of painting, following his sensibility to the tonality of colors. Thus, he could follow the variety of nature unhampered by the desire for regular forms that Raphael followed. A few years after he painted *The Bather,* Renoir wrote that everything that is beautiful is also irregular: Two eyes, when they are beautiful, are never entirely alike. Neither is a nose beautiful, when it is drawn exactly above the middle of the mouth. A segment of an orange, the foliage of a tree, the petals of a flower are never identical. Beauty of every description finds its charm in variety. Nature abhors both vacuum and regularity. For the same reason, no work of art can really be called such if it has not been created by an artist who believes in irregularity and rejects any set form. Regularity, order, desire for perfection (which is always a false perfection) destroy art. The only possibility of maintaining taste in art is to impress on artists and the public the importance of irregularity. Irregularity is the basis of all art.[1]

Looking at *The Bather* one can indeed understand how irregularity became Renoir's beauty, and how it was possible for him to follow with freedom and suppleness any variety of things as well as any nuance of light. Everything smiles from the canvas of Renoir, and a smile is the spontaneous expression of this happy adherence to nature and to its vibrating life. This is the individual as well as the universal beauty of Renoir's art.

But there is more to Renoir's pictorial beauty than that. One may go farther and try to understand some other aspects of it. Renoir's sense of universal beauty required of his work a looser finish than Raphael's painting did. His sense of monumentality was not expressed by contour lines like Raphael's, but through the volume of the body. The indetermination of the motif, which was neither a nymph nor a Madonna, but only a nude woman, freed Renoir's imagination from any extraneous limitation whether archæological or historical, and allowed him to think in terms of eternal beauty. Finally, this eternal beauty was no more and no less than the intimate caress the light created by Renoir bestowed on the things of earth.

Renoir led a Bohemian life to the end of his days in spite of the riches and renown which came to him in his later years. As a young man he often wandered through the streets

[1] L. Venturi, *Les Archives de l'Impressionnisme*, 1939, I, p. 128.

of Montmartre, the old Parisian center of artistic life, untidily dressed, absent-minded, and dreaming, entirely oblivious of what was going on around him. His movements were quick and his pace fast, but, in spite of his outward turmoil, his spirit was calm. While painting he would sing softly to himself gay melodies of his own creation. A young lady in love with him went so far as to describe him as "a poor boy, a body without soul" when he was not painting. Many believe that his voluptuousness and sensuality were what first awakened his artistic talent. It has been said that Renoir eulogized the breasts of women, and he himself once remarked: "If God had not created such beauty, I never should have become a painter." One day he would paint flowers while studying a nude model, and on another he would study flesh tones in a bouquet of roses. This sensuousness is partly responsible for Renoir's rendering of feminine charm in his artistic creations. But the wandering of his imagination, which was no doubt the cause of his absent-mindedness and day-dreaming, was also responsible for his going beyond feminine charm and for his realizing a charm of his own — that is, artistic charm. Everything smiles in his paintings: the eyes of a woman as well as the clothes she wears, a tree as well as a river, animate as well as inanimate things. It is the smile of sympathy and of participation in a cosmic life. And this is the greatness of Renoir's art.

In Chapter Six (fig. 30), we examined a painting by Toulouse-Lautrec closely allied to illustration and we took the opportunity of sketching the personality of the artist and the obviously close tie existing between his art and his life.

Both the illustrative character of that painting and the artistic integrity of the artist in his work may again be seen in figure 36, representing *The Clown Cha-U-Kao*. But the aim in this painting is different; in figure 30 a scene of vice is the object of reproduction, while in figure 36 beauty is the object. It is a thoroughly different kind of beauty from that which we find in the work of, say, Raphael, Ingres, or Renoir. But beauty, nevertheless.

To understand fully the quality of this painting it is well to remember what the French poet Baudelaire wrote in 1855 about the women painted by Delacroix: "One would say that they betray by their eyes a sorrowful secret, impossible to conceal even in the depth of dissimulation. Their wanness seems a revelation of interior struggles. . . . Such women, sick at heart or in mind, show in their eyes the black shadows of the fever or the abnormal phosphoresence of their sickness, and in their glance the intensity of surnaturalism." This was the romantic ideal of women's beauty in 1855. Now you must try to imagine yourself in 1895, the year of Toulouse-Lautrec's painting; in the so-called gay 'nineties — which alas were not gay at all, but a period full of unrest and discontent, seeking escape in a fury of amusements. The sickness of which Baudelaire spoke in 1855 had by 1895 gone farther, and had by then become a physical rather than a romantic sickness. Its moral strength, if sickness of body and soul can be called strength, lies in its own merciless self-exposure and its total lack of social and moral hypocrisy. As it has often been said, hypocrisy is the homage paid by vice to virtue. In the 'nineties, vice no longer cared to pay homage to virtue; it was sure of itself, and exhibited itself openly, thus claiming a virtue for itself — the virtue of sincerity. Toulouse-Lautrec was able to see in the dancers and clowns of the Moulin Rouge their sincerity even in their unhealthy appearance, and so painted them with spontaneous participation in their life and time. Moreover, he liked their artificiality and whim, and made of these a physical beauty. The costume of the clown Cha-U-Kao, as well as the rôle of Pierrette in which she is cast, both add to her artificiality; and Toulouse-Lautrec's line, nervous and incisive, was well adapted to portray this artificiality. Impressionism in general, and Renoir in particular, have always maintained a balance between naturalness and artificiality, between objective image and subjective style. But Post-Impressionism, to which Toulouse-Lautrec belonged, more and more accentuated artificiality and subjectivity. Being a clown, the image of Cha-U-Kao finds her naturalness in her own artificiality. And this is a typical characteristic of art. Thus the perfect naturalness both of the artificial beauty of the woman and the artificial style of the painter. Hence the exceptional grace of the image, of its personal traits, of its whimsical dress, and of the comic hints of theatrical surroundings. All these qualities can be summarized in a certain lightness of touch, which is the intimate quality of Toulouse-Lautrec's creative imagination, where motif and form find their perfect unity.

Vincent Van Gogh (1853–90) was born in Holland, the son of a Protestant minister from whom he inherited his great desire to preach, in everything he attempted: in business, religion, social reform and even in his private life, as well as in his art. This reforming zeal was, no doubt, the reason for the great difference between Van Gogh's style and the French art of his day—whose lack of preaching is not its least charming quality. Preaching in art is always a sign of bad taste, but Van Gogh's infinite energy and humility overcame all his shortcomings. He had the spirit of self-sacrifice and adoration—an adoration for everything he loved, peasants, trees, as well as his masters. Sometimes his scrupulousness in drawing resulted in his paying too much attention to details; his feeling was exaggerated rather than delicate; and his sentimentality often resulted in turbulent expression, but the turbulent expression at last gave way to free imagination. At that moment he found his serenity in forms and colors which would have been arbitrary had they not been impregnated with his excessive emotions.

So long as Van Gogh remained within the limits of his Dutch training, which was traditional and academic, his emotions did not, or could not, find perfect artistic expression. But after settling in Paris in 1886, four years before his death, he soon learned what the meaning of Impressionism was, how to use colors, and how to find a form adapted to the effect of colors. Thereafter he abandoned his preaching in paintings about social problems, and reduced his subject matters to motifs, the motifs of his vision. But after a year of research in the Impressionistic world, he went farther. He sympathized with Gauguin's trend towards a simplification of form and the reduction of light effects to a composition of color zones. This simplification was called "Symbolism." Forms and colors were no longer imagined as portraying an impression of nature, but as expressing a state of mind. They became the symbols of generalized emotions. A symbol is always an abbreviation of representation excluding all details, and can become a work of art only when the artist impresses on it a concentrated emotion. Van Gogh's emotions were of heroic stature, and so his simplification of form and color meant a concentration of expression. Besides, he loved pure, intense colors, with such a sensuous faith that his expression gained in evidence and striking force thereby. In his later years, such concentration of expression thoroughly absorbed his Christian and humanitarian feeling, thus resulting in a form of extreme vitality precisely because in his every touch of the brush his whole credo is contained.

Hence his greatness, which is distinct from that of any of his contemporaries. In his art he lacked the balance which favored the lovable naturalness of Renoir or the intellectual power of Cézanne, but he brought the trends of Impressionism and Symbolism to such extreme consequences that he discovered a new world for art. Of course, his works generally achieve a modern moral beauty rather than a physical beauty. But in figure 39 one can see that Van Gogh realized also a kind of physical beauty. It is a beauty very different from that of Raphael, even more remote than that of Renoir or of Toulouse-Lautrec. But it has neither the pagan attractiveness of Renoir nor the fanciful note of Lautrec. Without being a Madonna or a female saint, this beauty has none the less a Christian feeling. This derives from the fact that it is neither a nude nor a clown, but a peasant woman in her peasant costume, from the town of Arles. She is seated at a table, simply posing for her portrait. The motif is a natural one, belonging to the everyday life of a peasant and to the love for humble beings, which is essentially Christian.

172

Van Gogh's vision was more abstract than that of any artist before him. Neither plastic relief nor color-volumes interested him; only flat zones of color. Their relation to light and shade is only indirect. Their harmony is based on the contrast of colors, and this contrast lies essentially in the blues of the dress and the hair against the yellow background. Such harmony of colors without light and shade had been dismissed in painting since the fifteenth century. It is necessary to go back to Simone Martini (fig. 5) to find a harmony of the qualities of colors without regard to the effect of light. However, the latter's work has a gold background, symbol of Paradise. Van Gogh uses a yellow which can be painted on a wall, thus remaining within the limits of his experience of reality. Furthermore, it is true that the qualities of his colors are harmonized without regard to the effect of light, but the age-old experience of light and shade is not ignored by Van Gogh, while Simone Martini did not dream of it. That is, Van Gogh's qualities of color are distributed in those places where they have a symbolic function of light and shade. The white blouse and the blue dress of *The Arlesienne* have such function.

The beauty of this portrait of a woman from Arles, with its form in the shape of color zones, consists in its colors. Yet this abstract vision of color zones thoroughly realizes a natural image and it convinces us that both natural image and artistic vision were born together. The artist has created a new vision of reality, different from what we see in reality, but as convincing as reality itself, and coinciding with it in the infinite. This is the physical beauty of the image, and its value as pure art.

173

Chapter Nine

MODERN MORAL BEAUTY

IN Chapter Five we saw how luministic realism in the seventeenth century went beyond the mere representation of things to capture the soul of man in painting. In doing so, painting became more abstract, going beyond the mere reproduction of the physical aspects of reality by transforming them into light effects which themselves became the specific objects of painting. Thus physical beauty, both in single bodies and in compositions, was disregarded by the painters of this new luministic realism in order to attain a new kind of beauty, the beauty of the soul, which is moral beauty.

Later, in the nineteenth century, illustrators like Goya, Courbet, Toulouse-Lautrec (discussed in Chapter Six) realized a certain moral beauty in their paintings by using their luministic style to express their own political or social convictions in terms of art.

174

Fig. 40. DAUMIER: *Don Quixote and the Dead Mule*, 1868.

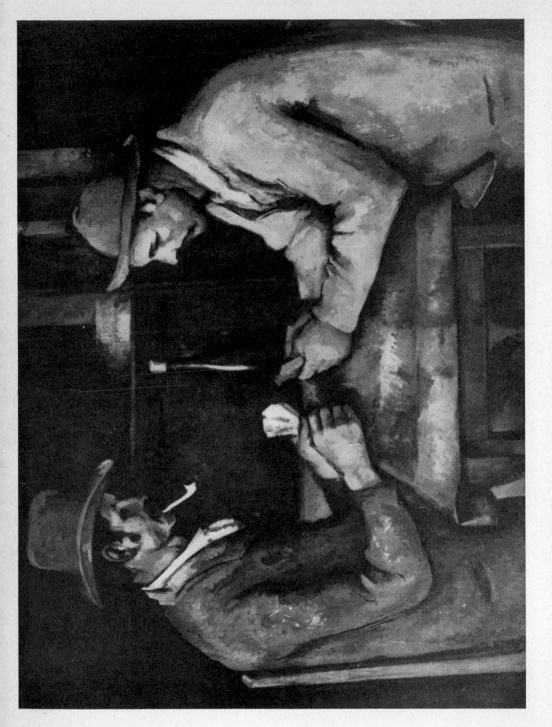

Fig. 41. CÉZANNE: *Card Players*, 1890-92.

Fig. 42. CÉZANNE: *The Gulf of Marseilles*, 1883–85.

Fig. 43. CÉZANNE: *Still-Life*, 1895–1900.

Fig. 44. VAN GOGH: *Bedroom at Arles*, 1889.

Fig. 45. ROUAULT: *The Old Clown*, 1917.

Fig. 46. ROUAULT: *The Crucifixion*, 1939.

At about the same time, during the nineteenth century, certain landscape painters (dealt with in Chapter Seven), working through their luministic style, attained a transformation of the physical appearance of nature with a freedom of imagination unknown before then, by conceiving their landscapes as "a state of mind." And not only that, but they realized also infinite new possibilities of pictorial light by using some colors as light, and some colors as shadow, independently of the sequence of white, gray, and black (which are not colors at all), thus identifying the effect of light with the effect of color.

Such an extraordinary development of the luministic style, along with its detachment from the physical aspects of nature, brought with it the necessity of transforming physical beauty to a point where its physical aspect became only secondary (see Chapter Eight) and opened the way to a new era of moral beauty.

The first painter to realize this new kind of moral beauty was Honoré Daumier (1808–79), one of whose masterpieces, *Don Quixote and the Dead Mule,* is reproduced in figure 40. This large watercolor was painted in 1868 expressly for his friend, the landscape painter, Daubigny.

Daumier had been for the greater part of his life a caricaturist in lithography and woodcut, and his powerful caricatures of prominent political figures and social events had won him great renown. Daumier was essentially an illustrator and, next to Goya, the greatest illustrator of the whole nineteenth century. But during the second half of his life his interest in caricature became less active, and he dedicated himself more and more to painting. Thereafter he lost his great popularity as a caricaturist, without acquiring during his lifetime any corresponding recognition of his real gift as a painter. And so he painted primarily to please himself and the few intimate friends who really appreciated his art, and, while almost starving as a man, he nevertheless enjoyed a freedom in painting, without any need for compromise, which was exceptional even in his day. Of course, many of the subjects of his paintings contain illustrative elements. The example reproduced in figure 40 was to illustrate Cervantes' famous novel, *Don Quixote*. But nothing remains in it of the illustration, for Daumier's form goes much farther than the mere representation of the specific subject matter of the novel, and attains its own independence by thoroughly embodying the artist's ideal.

Towards the top of the picture, behind the bony carcass of the dead mule and alongside the rotund Sancho, who is here prolonged by the form of his own mule, rises Don Quixote with his lance pointed up towards the sky. A few broken lines, a few suggestions of winy lilacs, of blues, grays, and browns, suffice to hint at the hero's lofty solitude. All human forms seem to disappear in this realm of abstract symbols, but without in the least losing in intensity and eagerness for life, so that they may come to express, almost beyond all association with known forms, a world of imagination, liberty, ideal aspiration, and heroic dignity, which is no doubt a finer dream than Don Quixote could probably ever have had — the very apotheosis of the popular hero elevated from the comic to the sublime.

Yet, notwithstanding the inspiration of Cervantes' novel,

176

no work of art is less illustrative than this magnificent water-color. Various elements of their art — their weapon of satire, their enthusiasm for the ideal of the heroic, and their familiarity with popular themes, manifested in the art of both men — link novelist and artist together. Yet, in spite of the artistic link, quite a distance· separates the *Don Quixote* of Daumier from that of Cervantes. Daumier's *Don Quixote* is a wholly new creation of romanticism, and there is expressed in it the artist's utter faith in his hero's ideal, feeling the grotesque as though it were the sublime, and seeing in the adventurer above all the martyr of an ideal. Whence an amazing zeal and earnestness. Here we may observe all that Daumier owes to Goya, both as a creator of symbols identifying the popular with the sublime, and as an initiator of ·the romantic style in painting. But at the same time we shall understand how the romantic conception of Don Quixote was realized by Daumier not only in a perfect and personal way, but by endowing it with a living force affecting us today. And we may also observe that in treating the symbols of the popular-sublime, Daumier went even farther than Goya did in freeing himself of naturalism, and in elevating it towards a purer and more coherent pictorial style.

His style was based on the effect of light and shade, and belonged to the same tradition as that of Goya and Rembrandt. However, because of the new conception of finish, *Don Quixote and the Dead Mule* resulted in being more of a suggestion than an affirmation of light and shade rendered by drawing. The drawing is here broken, there emphasized, elsewhere fading into nuances; it is open drawing, always susceptible to atmospheric variation. It is the drawing of a colorist, not the closed drawing of a plastic painter. Daumier's contemporaries clearly perceived his draughtsmanship was naturally colored, and that it evoked ideas of coloring, so intimately absorbed were the splendors of light and the depths of shade wrought in his drawing. From a logical point of view all this may appear as sheer nonsense. But feeling and imagination have a coherence of their own, which is parallel to the logic of thought, without identifying itself with it. One must realize that coloring, like plastic form and draughtsmanship, is, in art, a *way of feeling,* which changes according to time, place, and individuals. There is, for instance, the way of feeling draughtsmanship as a suggestion of color, as a color synthesized in light and shade, schematized in white and black; and there is the way of feeling draughtsmanship as contour spread out and graduated in order to transform a surface into a relief. The first way leads to pictorial form; the second, to plastic form. The first is Daumier's way, as it is the way of Titian, Rembrandt, and Goya. Thus Daumier, the draughtsman, perfectly realized his coloring in his drawing and initiated a new type of vision which in France contributed greatly to the development of modern art.

In the presence of Daumier's art, we ought to feel that his broken line and his ideal of the popular-sublime are but two aspects of the same artistic reality; and that their unity is the unity of Daumier's motif and form, the magic result of his sense of moral beauty, of his conception of pure art.

If one tries to personify modern moral beauty, he automatically thinks of Paul Cézanne (1839–1906). In fact, it would be hard to find a painter, whether old or modern master, where what is commonly called physical beauty is more often absent. At the same time it would be equally hard to find in the whole history of art a painter who, like Cézanne, could so abstract his style of form and color from any given experience of nature and yet convey through his abstractions so profound an interpretation of the nature of things, that every artist and also many laymen have in the last forty years seen nature with the eyes of Cézanne himself. Today, after thirty years of abstract art, we still find it quite difficult to answer the question as to whether Cézanne was a realist or an abstractionist. The truth is that his art, as all real art does, includes both nature and abstraction. And it is even possible to follow his creative process, which may be described as a journey from sensation of nature, identified with sensation of color, passing through subjective emotions on towards construction of abstract form. This first journey is from the object to the subject: that is, from the natural colors as they appear to the naked eye, to the emotions of the painter and the constructive power of his mind. Only by reaching this point can the painter master his own emotions as well as his color and sensations. But such a one-way journey would be without scope, the scope being the interpretation of nature, which also implies the return trip towards nature. The construction of abstract forms is not a scope in itself. The artist's purpose here is to interpret nature by stamping it with his own emotions and sensations. Abstract forms merely stress the essential elements of nature, selected by the artist's feelings and intelligence. A new nature is thus created, which is at the same time both objective and subjective:

179

that is, it is an artistic nature, capable of interpreting the essential aspects of what we see empirically in nature, "empirically" meaning "without intelligence."

All this we can find not only in the painting of Cézanne, but also in his letters.

"A keen sensation of nature—and certainly mine is quite keen—is the necessary basis for any conception of art on which depend the grandeur and beauty of all future work."

"Painters must devote themselves entirely to the study of nature. . . . One is never too scrupulous or too sincere or too submissive to nature."

He insists on the "idea . . . so sane, so comforting and the only correct one, of the development of art through contact with nature."

This "contact with nature" is based on color sensations. "I am very positive:—an optical impression is produced on our organs of sight which makes us classify as *light,* half-tone or quarter-tone the surfaces represented by color sensations. So that light does not exist for the painter. As long as we are forced to proceed from black to white, the first of these abstractions being like a point of support for the eye as much as for the mind, we are confused, we do not succeed in mastering ourselves, in *possessing ourselves.*"

Such color sensations are, however, a mere springboard for emotions, for, "As soon as you begin to feel yourself, your own emotions will finally emerge and conquer their place in the sun,—*get the upper hand,* confidence."

Emotions must be mastered, to be expressed, by the "good method of construction." "Treat nature by the cylinder, the sphere, the cone, everything in proper perspective so that each

180

side of an object or a plane is directed toward a central point. Lines parallel to the horizon give breadth, that is, a section of nature, or, if you prefer, of the spectacle that the Pater Omnipotens Aetherne Deus spreads out before our eyes. Lines perpendicular to this horizon give depth. But nature for us men is more depth than surface, whence the need for introducing into our light vibrations, represented by reds and yellows, a sufficient amount of blue to give the impression of air."[1]

Thus, in his own words, does Cézanne make clear for us his own creative process, which, from the sensation of colors, passes through his emotions, finally to reach the geometric construction of nature based on cylinder, sphere, and cone arranged in perspective. But once such construction is realized it is necessary to enliven it, as Cézanne does, by contrasting vibrating lights of reds and yellows with shadows of blue. So, the pictorial cycle is complete.

We can now better understand Cézanne's relation to Impressionism. The beginning of his creative process is color sensation, like that of the Impressionists; and, as with them, the emotional response is along the same line. The end of the process, which is the realization of nature through the contrast of red, yellow, and blue, is also thoroughly impressionistic. What the Impressionists lacked was that middle point — construction and geometrical ideal — where Cézanne's intellectual power found the essential element of style. This was the skeleton Cézanne wanted in order to support and co-

[1]Paul Cézanne, *Letters*. London, 1941. 1904, January 25, April 15, May 26, December 9 and 23. 1906, September 13. The translation from the French has been twice changed.

ordinate his sensibility. And because of this skeleton he was able to give his sensation both a simplified form and an independence of nature unknown before. The skeleton functioned as a distinguishing principle between the work of art and nature — hence his freedom of imagination. At the same time, by his way of convincing the spectator concerning the naturalness of his imagination, he created a world apart, a living world parallel to, but not identical with, nature — the world of art itself.

The universal success of Cézanne's art depends on the fact that both his abstraction and his naturalness coincide with the best results of modern theory of art. The idea of art has had to surmount many obstacles throughout the centuries before finding its own way to a convincing truth. At the beginning, it was said that art is an imitation of nature; later, it came to be understood as a creation of man. But many painters stuck to the idea of imitation. Cézanne's independence of any imitation of nature is only too evident. Then sensation in art was disregarded, and art was believed to be a mental construction with as little sensation in it as possible. Cézanne's mental construction was only the skeleton of a living image, living because thoroughly impregnated by sensation. Then imagination was considered the essential instrument of art, even if detached from any appearance of reality, but the working of Cézanne's powerful imagination was used only to penetrate the eternal aspects of nature. Then the religious, moral, political, and, in general, illustrative aspects of art were emphasized at the expense of the autonomy of art — hence the importance assigned to the subject matter. But Cézanne by starting from sensation radically destroyed any subject matter, thus creating a form adapted to the motif of his emotions, and to nothing else. This is the reason why Cézanne's art has appeared for forty years the purest art that history records.

How Cézanne's creative process was realized in his paintings can be summarily shown by the three following examples:

The *Card Players* (fig. 41) is a composition of figures. The structure of forms based on the composition of masses of colors has nothing to do with anatomical structure. For instance, Cézanne has no desire to show in this picture the connection of the hand with the arm of the player. The arm is covered by a sleeve showing the connection between the hand and the sleeve, but not between the hand and arm. It is a relationship of tone and volume, not of anatomy, like the relationship existing between a face and a hat. The vision here being from without, realization progresses from appearance to reality. Anatomical knowledge being a vision from within, a painter can take advantage of it in the structure of a human body, but not in a relationship between a table and a man. The unity of Cézanne's style depends on the composition of light and color, which form a table in the same way that they do a man, realizing volumes that occupy space in depth without chiaroscuro relief. Everything lives and breathes in that atmosphere of color and light, which is the realm of pictorial atmosphere. Every detail is enlivened by that atmosphere; that is to say, a man or a pipe does not exist as such for its own sake, but as an element of the painting as a whole. It is the whole which gives the unity of style and which justifies all details.

Cézanne was aware that "The color sensations, which give

light, also cause abstractions which — when the points of contact are tenuous and delicate — do not allow me either to cover my canvas or to follow to the end the delimitation of the objects." (October 23, 1905.) In order to explain this point, we can do no better than to have recourse to a happy distinction he himself suggested: "No modelling but modulation." According to the original meaning, to model is "to impress a body" and to modulate is to move the voice through intervals. The ensemble of a figure or composition by Cézanne is produced not by a material connection but by rhythm: that is, one part of the picture is not connected with another according to the drawing, but according to the relation between the surfaces of colors. "Painting," he said, "is not slavishly to copy the subject: it is to find a harmony between numerous relations." The unity born of such relations is not a material one, but an image created by the imagination.

"To see into nature is to separate the character from the model." That is, Cézanne wanted to represent neither the bodies of the players, nor the table, nor the bottle, but the character of the two peasants, with their natural environment. Of course their character was what the artist felt to be the truth about them. He once said: "I admire above all the appearance of people who have grown old naturally, and live according to the laws of their age. Look at this old innkeeper. What an air! Then look at this shop girl who is very attractive indeed. But in her coiffure and in her clothes, what falsehood!" Cézanne recognized nobility of style not in the conventional untruths or half-truths of society, called idealizing, but in the frank sincerity of a commonplace reality that is true to life. Compare these peasants with those of Millet

184

(fig. 27), who refined them to make them acceptable to the upper classes, and you will instantly see what "to be true to life" means for Cézanne and for art. A portrait of a peasant by Cézanne is as individualized as the peasant himself and yet universal as an idea, solemn as a monument, and firm as moral consciousness. This is moral beauty of the highest degree.

The same principles and the same sensibility that produced the *Card Players* were also instrumental in producing *The Gulf of Marseilles* (fig. 42). From the hills in the village of Estaque, Cézanne could see a wonderful panorama with many picturesque elements, but he deliberately eschewed both the panorama and the picturesque. The relationship between the various zones of color, in light or in shadow, was too necessary, too insistent under the aspect of eternity, to allow him to enjoy the irregularity of the picturesque. A comparison with a landscape by Pissarro (fig. 35) explains what Cézanne has in common with his master insofar as the impressionistic vision goes. Both paintings are based on color and sensations, but the variety of sensations, which is very rich in Pissarro, prevents him from elaborating on color. Of course, in Pissarro, too, there is unity of style, but this has neither the severe coherence nor the extreme simplification which Cézanne has. The picturesque has not been thoroughly absorbed in the pictorial, and above all the structure, though existing, is not so imposing as in Cézanne. In Pissarro there is more charm; in Cézanne more grandeur.

Cézanne's incomparable chromatic splendor, its intensity, restfulness, and firmness, depend on the same qualities as does his form. Pissarro used color-relations of light and shadow as

Cézanne did, even going so far as to teach Cézanne the use of them. But since the effect of color is dependent on its form, and the variety of elements in Pissarro is so great, a certain dispersion is felt both in form and color harmony. On the other hand, the emphasis placed by Cézanne on the structure of his elements is responsible for the width of the color zones, and for the simplification and strength of the harmony. He was conscious of the primary importance of relations: "There is neither light nor dark painting; there are simply tone relations. When these are realized correctly, harmony is automatically established."

For the sake of structure Cézanne also avoided the panoramic character of the view before him. The mountains in the background are about eight miles distant from the Estaque. But as he wished to represent them in their structure, he got closer to them. But at the same time he also wanted to maintain the relationship between the houses of the Estaque and the distant mountains. How could he? By simply representing the foreground in the painting as more distant than it actually is in nature. So he abstracted both the foreground and the background in the painting from their actual position in nature. In this way Cézanne avoided any suggestion as to the place he occupied in the hills of the Estaque while painting the picture, thus keeping himself entirely outside the vision realized in the picture. He treated the surface of the sea similarly. He took advantage of the fact that from a high ground the surface of the sea seems to surge upward, suggesting a big volume of water. And because of the massiveness of the sea, it is easy to imagine that the mountains beyond that mass of water are distant even if their clear structure corresponds to nearer objects. We can say that such a sea is neither far nor near, but only a relationship between the mountains and the village. All this was a deliberate abstraction from the subjective reality of the painter. The actual view was detached from what Cézanne had literally before his naked eyes, in order to organize an objective relation of village, sea, and mountains. And as a work of art, it is sufficient in itself that the surfaces are interrelated and have their own imaginative explanation. Hence the representation is perfectly objective, not in relation to nature, but to art. In nature, "near" and "far" are material terms in a finite world. Cézanne's work is so coherent, so self-sufficient, that it belongs to no particular world: it is a world unto itself, dwelling in the Infinite and in the Universal, with the solemnity of things which eternally endure.

Cézanne endowed still-life — a not-important genre before him — with a strong impulse, and gave it an entirely new significance. Still-life in painting means representation of inanimate things, such as fruit and furniture. Of course, inanimate things have always been used as subjects in painting for the purpose of adding ornament to a composition of human figures. But it was very rarely that inanimate things were chosen as the only motif of a painting, without human figures, until modern realism appeared between the end of the sixteenth century and the beginning of the seventeenth century. Then it became a genre new in painting, long despised as pure imitation of unworthy phases of nature and as lacking any ideal values at all. But in spite of often-repeated objections and condemnations, still-life gained world renown in recent years, because of Cézanne's art. When interest in story-telling in painting diminished or disappeared altogether, in order to emphasize the artist's style, a still-life drew its special interest from the lack of interest shown in its subject matter. That is, the modern painter found in apples, for example, the best motif for his painting, precisely because it was the simplest one, and so he reduced to a minimum the subject matter in order to attain an absolute liberty of style and express his own state of mind by lines, forms, and colors only. This detachment of art from the thing represented was realized to the utmost in the still-life. And people began to say that old painters portrayed Madonnas, and the new ones portrayed apples. Furthermore, they said that modern painters had reduced inspiration to an interest in inanimate things. This was untrue: the reverse was true. Freedom of imagination had attained in modern painting such force, that even an apple became a proper vehicle for an artist's desire for the sublime. In actual life, sublimity in an apple would be ridiculous. But in pictorial life everything is possible. It is possible, of course, only if the painter considers an apple as a pretext for realizing his lines, forms, and colors, and abstains from portraying his apples in a realistic way. The same problem faces the realist when portraying a man; if he reproduces all aspects of his figure to perfection, then he ceases to be an artist, and becomes a mere hand-photographer. And in the case of an apple, even more so, because the photograph of an nature of a hero rather than that of a man.

Figure 43 reproduces a *Still-Life* by Cézanne where inanimate objects are transformed into a cosmic tragedy. The reduction of the fruits, the glass, the pitcher, etc., to light and shade, volumes and colors, is so radical that nobody will notice the objects. This is true abstract art, having a life of its own, independent of nature as well as of literary or historical subject matter. But it is not an art abstract from sensation and emotion. Schemes of cylinders and cones may exist underneath. But the result, the painted surface above all, reveals an emotional energy of epic and sublime stature — the nature of a hero rather than that of a man.

Is this an unfinished painting? That is an amazing question when we recall what Cézanne said in 1874: "I still must work, not to put on the final polish which imbeciles admire. What is commonly appreciated is only manual skill, which renders all work resulting from it inartistic and common. I must strive after perfection only for the pleasure of painting with more truth and wisdom." Now we can understand why Cézanne left his still-life "unfinished." A fully realized volume of fruits would have diminished his dramatic expression.

Monumental grandeur, moral consciousness, the universal idea found in a portrait of peasants, the solemnity of things which eternally endure found in a landscape, a cosmic tragedy expressed by a still-life — all this is the moral beauty of Cézanne's art. And now, think again of Rembrandt and his *Supper in Emmaus:* here is a moral beauty tied to a religious conception of Christ. Cézanne was a faithful Christian. But the Christian aspect of his art is lateral. He is the son of romanticism, a worshiper of nature, of the common people, of the common things of everyday life. But he is also a seer who can see in a peasant, in the surface of the sea, in some fruit, eternal and universal values, beyond the confines of any formal religion. Hence the incomparable greatness of his art.

Figure 44 reproduces *Bedroom at Arles,* a still-life, by Van Gogh, which was described by the artist himself as being: "Just simply my bedroom, only here color is to do everything, and, giving by its simplification a grander style to things, is to be suggestive here of *rest* or of sleep in general. In a word, to look at the picture ought to rest the brain or rather the imagination. The walls are pale violet. The ground is of red tiles. The wood of the bed and chairs is the yellow of fresh butter, the sheets and the pillows very light greenish lemon. The coverlet scarlet. The window green. The dressing table orange. The basin blue. The doors lilac. And that is all — there is nothing in the room with closed shutters. The broad lines of the furniture again must express inviolable rest. Portraits on the walls and a mirror and a towel and some clothes. This by way of revenge for the enforced rest I was obliged to take. I shall work at it all day, but you see how simple the conception is. The shadows and the shadows thrown are suppressed; it is painted in free flat washes like the Japanese prints."[1]

The color is very intense, without shadows, with some colors symbolizing shadow and others symbolizing light. This simplification of the effect of light and shade to pure symbols is suggestive of strong emotional power. The form too is simplified, to such a point that the impression is merely summarily perceived. The form is only a shape, what corresponds to the light and shade being only flat colors. Thus the perfect unity of form and color.

The subject matter is Van Gogh's bedroom in Arles. It is a still-life — but Van Gogh himself knew how to distinguish

[1]*Letters,* 1886–89, London, 1929, p. 234.

between his subject matter and his motif. He says that it suggests: *rest* and *sleep*. This is his motif. He had been ill and obliged to remain there. "By way of revenge for the enforced rest" he painted this picture. He sees a poor sunny room, and he feels that the things themselves are asleep. The room itself emanates a feeling of loneliness excluding any suggestion of the presence either of Van Gogh or of any other human being. But the things in the room express something more than sleep — they were abandoned. And they were abandoned in such a careless state as to give the suggestion of disorder. Hence a magic value of something real, felt, and yet immaterial, as of eternal abandonment, departure, or death — a hint of tragedy.

At that time Van Gogh was sad and discouraged, still passionately attached to his work, and longing for salvation. He wanted to portray sleep, but he could not. The approaching tragedy of a mind becoming unbalanced thwarted his rest and sleep. In the abandoned room there is calm, but a calm without hope, and without surcease. The colors are brilliant and intense, but they do not suggest joy, only sadness. So that this "rest" born of distress and these sunny colors born of sadness give the mood a sweetness, an innocence, and a grace which are religious in import. They express the intimate state of mind of the painter, in spite of himself. In his letters he is not aware of it. And because he is not aware of it, he achieves a form where all his hope and good nature are evident. Thus the expression is not immediate and direct, but mediate and indirect. In passing from the feeling to the expression something has been found: the form of rest and sunny colors. And it is this form which gives to the expression of feeling the value of art. It is this form which may be called the moral beauty of Van Gogh's art.

George Rouault (born in 1871) has attained in his painting a moral beauty so opposite to any physical beauty that no other painter in modern times has been able even remotely to approach him. To understand why this has happened it is necessary to go back to Goya, Daumier, Cézanne, and Van Gogh in order to remember that in the nineteenth century moral beauty was identified with the lot of the common people as a reaction against physical beauty, which had by tradition been identified with the upper classes. This finding of the salvation of the soul in the lower classes, in the simplicity of life, in a subverted sublime, was the claim of nineteenth-century painting, one of the greatest contributions to art of all time. This love for poor people, this ability to feel in them absolute moral values, was essentially Christian, and gave birth to the only really religious art of that time, even if it was not recognized as such by the Catholic Church. At the end of the nineteenth century and at the beginning of this present one, a new revival of religious feeling took place in France, and certain writers as well as painters were even more deeply concerned with religion than with social problems. The common man was considered the real creature of God, but, what was even more significant, the actual goal of these painters and writers was God Himself. No modern painter has manifested such strong religious impulses as has Rouault in his art. He is the only modern exponent of a great art which is at the same time a religious art. In comparison with the art of the preceding century, which extolled the virtues of the common people, Rouault's art has less social meaning, but attains to values which have a universal religious significance.

The Catholic Church, which has thus far failed to recognize the Christian import of Rouault's art, has so far also failed to recognize Rouault's mentor in Christianity, the writer Léon Bloy, because both are against Christian civilization and for "Christian barbarism." Bloy fulminated against "people who glory in their respectability, in other words, weak and clinging monsters, who are equally incapable of the abominations of vice or virtue." Similarly, Rouault flatly refuses to demean himself by painting refined figures of seraphim, angels, and Madonnas acceptable to the Church. He sees the world around him as it actually is, and he is too honest with himself and towards his art to conceal his natural reactions. Seeing ugliness and crime all around him, he condemns the world he lives in, and puts into his condemnation such grandeur, strength, and violence — such a universal meaning — that it becomes a religious condemnation. To do this it was necessary for Rouault to be free of any dogmatic limitation. As a man he is far from being a rebel. On the contrary, he is a faithful observant of Catholic doctrine, but all the power and sincerity of his reaction to the world about him is in his painting. Thus he goes back to the original sources of religious faith, to rediscover faith at whatever risk to the present world, to recognize a God anterior to the idea of Satan. His faith is not mere enlightened choice: it is a force of nature.

In 1937 he wrote: "I am obedient, but it is within the province of everyone to revolt; it is more difficult to obey silently certain inner urges and to pass one's life searching for

sincere and appropriate means of expression for our temperament and our talent, if we have any." Rouault is a keen psy-
chologist with a deep insight into human nature and a very
subtle discernment for all that is hypocritical, pharisaical, and
false, awakening in him a very deep and violent repugnance.
Another strong tendency of his is to fling himself "into the
heart of the fray" and to sacrifice himself, not for some long-
cherished ideal, but for some powerful instinctive impulsion
of the moment. Thus, after having pried open all the secrets
of the best academic training, he instinctively chose a new
direction which came from an "urgent inner impulse, from
a . . . penetrating vision and from the need to approach
religious subjects in a manner free of hypocritical convention."

Thus, as an act of destiny he became a rebel in art. And
when he finally saw his pictures hung in exhibitions he
found them "frightening," while the public found them "out-
rageous." Evidently he believed that the academic manner
he had been taught was as false as the world he condemned.
Finish, beauty, subtle outline, chiaroscuro, nuance, illusion
of space, everything was false and hypocritical. He studied
Degas, Lautrec, Cézanne, but rejected for himself everything he had studied. He went straight to the images born
of his imagination—images which seem as though belonging
to another planet. And by disregarding all rules of painting
and anterior experiences of life, he became a primitive master.
A painting of his seems sketched in a few minutes, whereas
in actuality it might have been reworked scores of times over
a period of years.

The Old Clown (fig. 45) is a good example of the artistic
form of Rouault. The nose, the mouth, the eyes are roughly

painted; but any refinement would have destroyed the form of the whole. The face and cap have a completely oval shape, but that shape is alive because of its rough features and the sharp interruptions of shadows: without them, it would be a conventional painting; with them, it is as powerful in plasticity as it is original in expression. The shadows are often zones of black tints, being not only shadows but functioning also as sharp contrasts to the intense colors, which function as light. Thus lights and shadows serve both as depth for plasticity and as surface for coloring. Such simplification of means is carried to its extreme, not for the sake of simplification, as in the case of a "primitivist," but for the purpose of intensifying the expression, as with a genuine primitive master. Clowns have been the life-long dream of Rouault, who has loved them since early youth because of their poverty and sadness, and because they too are artists in their own way, and transcend the misery of their private lives to attain the free fancy of the artist. Moreover, he envies their wandering about the world, while he feels pinned down to his static job of painting, like a peasant to his field. He has painted clowns scores of times, always emphasizing their sadness as well as their ornaments and fanciful colors, thus expressing their humanity not only as men but also as clowns. Their being clowns makes possible their participation in art, and Rouault finds in their art an indirect way to express their humanity. Thus the image of a clown becomes an image of piety, of religious piety. With some slight changes in his features, this clown could easily become an image of the suffering Christ. The fact is that in almost any of Rouault's images the expression is the same: human sympathy for universal suffering. And it is this sympathy, this participation, this generosity which gives form to the suffering.

Rouault's *Crucifixion* (fig. 46) expresses his religious feeling directly through the image of God. The sorrow of St. John at right and of the Madonna at left are powerfully represented. Yet theirs are hardly human faces: it is their general attitudes towards the sacred figure on the cross, emblazoned by big black lines under the chin, which are responsible for the expression. The form can hardly be more abstract. But the abstract lines are so impressed with the artist's tremendous emotional intensity that their power is inescapable. Compare Rouault's *Crucifixion* with the thirteenth-century *Head of Christ* (fig. 3) or with Berlinghieri's *St. Francis* (fig. 4): these forms also are abstract, but less expressive of emotion. Of course, the despair of Rouault's image is neither analyzed nor specified; it is despair in general, but this does not diminish its force. Charged with despair, the Christ on the cross is not an image of piety but of reverence. Hence, grandeur and monumentality. Old masters elevated the cross in their paintings in order to emphasize the monumentality of the image. Not Rouault; his Christ is erected on the ground: it is the ample chest and the erect head which give a feeling of monumentality to the whole image. He is the King, the Saviour, and His arms seem thrown open for the protection of the faithful, rather than nailed to the cross.

Thus, the extreme simplicity of Rouault's artistic form reveals the extreme intensity of his feeling—of his emotional participation in the universal sorrow of mankind and in man's reverence for God. Such simplicity is the result of a great revolt against a sophisticated world as well as against a sophisticated tradition of art. Rouault's rebellion against both social and artistic traditions was at the root of his discovery of a new form. Hence, the extraordinary value of his form of moral beauty.

Chapter Ten

ABSTRACT AND FANTASTIC ART

THE WORKS of art treated in this chapter are by living painters, and represent some of the best achievements of our time. As they are the result of different artistic temperaments and of contrasting theories, they bear no resemblance to one another either in form or content. Yet they have something in common: an aversion to nature and a longing for an absolute form of art, beyond sense experience and reasoning. The only living painter we have examined so far is Rouault, whose reaction to nature was a search for an absolute — an absolute, however, still rooted in Christianity. But the painters dealt with in this chapter want to go beyond even that: they want to reach the absolute independently of any traditional religion or philosophy, they try to destroy all cherished conventions of seeing and thinking — hence the world around them as it has been seen and thought since the

198

Fig. 47. SCHOOL OF PIERO DELLA FRANCESCA: *Perspective*, c. 1470.

Fig. 48. PICASSO: *The Red Tablecloth*, 1924.

Fig. 49. PICASSO: *A Woman Writing*, 1923.

Fig. 50. BRAQUE: *Platter of Fruit*, 1925.

Fig. 51. MATISSE: *Odalisque with Tambourine*, 1926.

Fig. 52. MARIN: *Pertaining to Stonington Harbor, Maine, 1926.*

Fig. 53. CHAGALL: *The Martyr*, 1940.

beginning of man—in order to rebuild a world of their own, by pure inventive imagination. To say that they are right or wrong in their rebellion against tradition is not the point when one tries to understand their paintings. What is important is to find out how thoroughly was their philosophy absorbed by their imagination, how sensitive and emotional was their imagination, and how successfully was it realized in visual forms and colors. In other words, the artistic personalities of contemporary painters must be judged as we judge the artistic personalities of painters of any time, accepting all the data they offer us, as far as their aims and means are concerned, and checking their results to see whether or not they belong to eternal art. This point ought to be emphasized when we approach contemporary art, rather than when we look at paintings of the past. In fact, so many controversies arose over the theories of Cubism and Surrealism that bias concerning these theories frequently veils the unique problem of an art critic, which is to decide whether by virtue of Cubism and Surrealism, or in spite of them, a painting is a work of art or not.

The following exposition of some of the ideologies held by contemporary painters has therefore the purpose of introducing the reader into their world. We shall try not to misjudge them as ideologies, but any conclusion concerning the value of an artist must perforce ultimately depend on the analysis of his paintings.

At the beginning of our century, a reaction took place against Realism and Impressionism as trends adhering too faithfully to nature. To find the essence, the truth, the absolute in art, the new painters began to distort the shape of things, and then to invent new shapes which were independent, sometimes absolutely independent, of any natural shape. Such a trend is known as "abstract art."

In the history of philosophy, the idea of abstraction has undergone constant change throughout the centuries. Plato considered universal truth as ideas abstracted from reality, but Aristotle, by giving ideas only a formal value, brought truth back to reality, and opposed abstraction. In modern times, Kant distinguished pure concepts from empirical ones in the following way; pure concepts, being universal, are *the process of abstracting* from sensations; only empirical concepts *are* abstract rather than abstracting *from* sensations. And recently Husserl emphasized the inseparability of fact and essence, of the concrete and the abstract. The exigency of uniting idea and fact, of considering idea, not abstract from reality, but immanent in it, has dominated the main trend of modern philosophy.

In æsthetics, the problem of abstraction has been complicated by the ancient definition of art as imitation of nature. Abstraction was then conceived as an idealization of nature attained through a choice in nature. From Plotinus on through the Middle Ages, in æsthetics the concept of nature was ignored and artistic form was conceived as a relative beauty emanating from absolute beauty, God, and was thus absolutely abstract from nature. But since the Renaissance, art has again become connected with nature and is considered as an interpretation of nature by the imagination of the artist, and thus abstracting from nature and not completely separate and detached from it. On the other hand, the new emphasis put on the senses, and the new concept of taste, substituted the senses of the artist for nature, as reality in art. Reality, being subjective, was then no longer nature but the senses. And abstraction—that is, the style of the artist— meant abstracting from the senses and not from nature. Every work of art was considered at the same time both abstract and concrete, its concreteness consisting of the sensations, and its abstractness consisting of the universal values emanating from the representation of sensations.

Today when we speak of *abstract art* we mean cubism and its variations. The painters who invented cubism and the critics who supported it were not well versed in philosophy, and they therefore ignored the new ideas on æsthetics concerning the reality of art as consisting of the sensations of the artist. They craved a reaction against nature; yet, while anxious to be free of nature, they thought always, paradoxically, in terms of nature. They therefore created an image of something which was the very opposite of nature without being aware that the opposite of nature is on the same level with nature, and not on the level of art.

This polemical character of cubism has been well expressed by the poet, Guillaume Apollinaire. He says:

"Plastic virtues, purity, unity and truth trample on an already prostrate nature.

"Above all the only true artists are those who wish to become inhuman, and try to find symbols of inhumanity, symbols which cannot be found in nature. These symbols are for them the truth and in none other do they recognize reality." Cubist painters "wishing to attain the proportions of an ideal (which means a geometrical ideal) without being limited by humanity, create works which are more cerebral than sensible.

"Picasso studies an object as a surgeon dissects a corpse."[1]

These passages show a continual change of thought from opposition to nature to hatred of sensibility. Inhumanity, ratiocination, and dissection of corpses became the main approach to art. Therefore, this kind of abstract art is not only opposite to nature, but it is also thoroughly abstract from man and his sensibility.

To all this must be added that at the beginning of our century a crisis was noted in the conclusions of science, which was no longer sure of its concepts based on pure logic alone, of its mathematical truths. So the new painters felt free to use science for their own purposes and to believe in their own scientific achievements without in the least caring for the skeptical attitude of sound criticism or for the control of logic. Their science was only a starting point for the free play of their imagination. What they wanted was to reach an ideal that would embrace the "infinite universe," but having cut themselves off completely from their experiences of the surrounding world, they eventually ended up in a vacuum, where they had to be contented with their innate power of mystic suggestion, and were forced to admit their objective impotence, their negation of any objective ideal.

This was the program of cubism; and the following summary is an attempt to give an idea of the way it was finally realized in practice: An object has always been represented from only one point of view, but the cubists wanted to represent it from many sides. So they cut it into parts, reduced each part to its simplest form, which is approximately a geometric form, and juxtaposed the other parts like projections of the

[1]Guillaume Apollinaire, *Les Peintres Cubistes,* 1913, pp. 5, 10, 14, 18.

first one. Then they transposed on the surface of their painting all elements which in their perspective arrangement had represented space in depth. This dissection of an object into parts, and their arrangement on the surface, was an attempt to suggest both the view of the object from all possible sides and the exposition of its parts on the surface. The result, of course, was that human perception of the object utterly failed, and that an interpretation was needed to reconstruct in the imagination the dissected object. The arrangement of the parts of the object, which were partly geometric and partly verisimilar in form, followed the geometric projections only partially, and generally was due to free imagination. If this imagination was arbitrary, that is, detached from the senses, the result was a failure. But if the imaginative arrangement included a pattern, a sense of proportion —a sense of balance, of relation between form and color, of harmony of colors and so on—then the result could reveal the personality of the painter, his interest in life; how, for example, he felt, loved, and hated. Then the result would be a work of art.

Generally speaking, a painter feels his motif, and expresses himself through the motif, going from the concrete to the abstract, that is, from feeling to style. In this, cubist painters made use of a double process: going from the concrete to the abstract and back again to the concrete. But their process of abstracting from the object was not an artistic one. It was a cool, logical calculation, a purely mechanical process. When, however, they found themselves confronted with their artificial abstractions, and, if they were real artists, decided to let their imagination work in a concrete way, then they came down to earth and began to wrestle in earnest with the reality of their feeling, sometimes achieving a real work of art.

Now please look at *The Red Tablecloth* by Picasso (fig. 48), one of the most renowned, and the easiest to understand, of all his semi-abstract paintings. It is a still-life, representing a table covered by a red cloth, a sheet of music, a guitar, a fruit-dish with a slice of melon on it, a sculptured head, and a large window in the background. The cubistic method is evident in the projections of the guitar and the fruit-dish, in the juxtaposition of the zones of light and shade, like patterns which are independent of the representation of the table, and in the linear features of the head. That is, this still-life has an indirect relation to a natural still-life; it has a unity of lines, forms, and colors, an organism of its own, and a unity of style. The formal relation of the sheet of music, of the fruit-dish and the melon, of the lines of the head and the window, of the decoration of the guitar and the cloth, and so on, contribute to the unity of the scene; while the arrangement of colors accentuates that unity. The upper part of the picture is painted in very bright colors: the window is white, sky-blue, and, a small section of it, very light gray; the melon and bowl are white, with some very transparent green, violet, pink, and yellow; and the sheet of music is white and black. All of these are framed by colors which are very strong and dark, beginning with the black marble head on the brown table, the red-and-black cloth, and the brown-and-black guitar. The dark color zones give the impression of great monumentality, of plastic stability; while the bright color zones express the free flight of the artist's imagination from darkness towards light.

At this point, we may well ask: What is abstract in this painting? And what is the character of this abstraction?

Figure 47 shows a composition of architectonic space in *Perspective* by a follower of Piero della Francesca, painted in the fifteenth century. It is an abstract painting. Its abstraction does not consist in the fact that it does not represent anything. On the contrary, it represents some columns, some houses, a street, and some boats in the background. However, it is abstract because the geometric forms and the perspective lines dominate the representation of the scene to such an extent that nothing is left of the freedom and variety of man and nature. It is a cold rigid architecture, if you will — but still a mathematical scheme of space. Here the painter first made his calculation of perspective, and then covered it with the most appropriate buildings he could design to demonstrate his calculation. All this could very well be a scholastic exercise in geometry, but how could it become art? The painter loved something — empty space in perspective, emphasized by the porch in the foreground, and gave to this empty space something of magic, the sense of things fixed for eternity. His belief or illusion that perspective could impress things with the sense of eternity, of universality, and of absoluteness is the artistic seal of this painting.

If now we leave the follower of Piero della Francesca and go back to Picasso, we shall soon become aware that the latter has no faith at all in science and uses geometric elements capriciously, occasionally only, sticking to arbitrary forms, in relation both to science and nature. Still, there is in Picasso a necessity for abstraction, in order to follow certain rhythms of his own in pattern and color. It is an abstraction born of the imagination, and, as always happens in abstractions, the only possibility in it for art is to induce a vague feeling of contemplation for the eternal, the universal, and the absolute. That is, in the fifteenth as in the twentieth century, abstract painting could realize a contemplative world, without distinctions, without emotions, but still capable of a rarefied life, which is art.

On the other hand, there is proof that such kind of contemplation is indigenous to Picasso's imagination. *A Woman Writing* (fig. 49) was painted in 1923, one year before *The Red Tablecloth*. There are no cubistic elements in it, no deformations, no projections. As far as the subject matter is concerned nothing could be more realistic. However, even this painting is an abstract one suggesting, as it does, not any real woman, but the portrait of an image, with neither the woman nor the artist doing anything but exhibiting, the one an appealing pose, and the other a superb drawing, both as devoid of life as a fossil. They both may be said to belong to another planet. And a simple man looking at a painting like this one can only contemplate, a little astonished, what must seem to him an image fixed for eternity, having the character of the universal and the absolute, but totally lacking in any of those human imperfections which belong to concrete human life. Thus, when Picasso uses his cubistic tools or when he follows traditional forms of painting he is always abstract.

But let us here digress from him as an artist and look at the man himself. A Spaniard, Picasso was born in 1881, and since early youth has been drawing with a natural skill for mastering technique rare at any time. He said: "I have difficulty in understanding the meaning of research. I do not seek. I find." This is perfectly true: his facility in achieving what he wants is the result of this exceptional mastery of technique. In fact, he could very easily have become a successful academic painter. But as he is a very serious and faithful artist, he could not waste his great talent on such questionable worldly success. Believing that art is invention, he has during a lifetime of furious activity changed his style of painting many times in obedience to the impulse of the moment to invent something new. He "does not seek," he "finds." But what he finds is always something unexpected and amazing. This is due to the quick workings of his decisive mind in immediate compliance with his impulses. But he never thinks of integrating his new achievements with those of the past, nor even with his own previous achievements. And when inspired by motifs drawn from the past, he changes them so radically that nothing remains of them in his painting but the realization of his ideas held at that particular moment. Picasso is no more moderate as a man than he is as an artist. In fact, he deliberately ignores moderation, and is often contradictory and violent in his opinions as he is in his art. But everything he does he affirms with unshaken assurance, with terrific authority. This is the secret of his artistic success and fame. No painter since the death of Cézanne has had such tremendous influence on other painters as Picasso has had.

All these forceful elements in Picasso's character are no doubt favorable to a conqueror, to an inventor, perhaps to an executive. But are they favorable to an artist? We all know, or should know, that an essential difference exists between the inventor and the creator, and that the artist is, above all, a creator. An inventor may invent or discover some new object or gadget useful to humanity, say the airplane, the radio or the safety-razor. A creator, on the other hand, does not discover anything outside himself. What he puts into his painting or his poem must come from within himself. And the artistic value of the object he has made — the canvas painted or the book written — consists exactly in his making the object capable of revealing his own personality or personal values, which are beyond the measuring rod of science or mechanical formulæ.

Picasso's habit of finding without seeking, and his over-hasty decisions often result in ambiguities of judgment and selection. As the late English art critic, Roger Fry, once observed, his reactions to vision are both "diverse and uncertain." Sentimental motifs and plastic abstractions do not converge at the same point, but proceed along parallel lines that never meet. Hence the opposite, and often conflicting, traits we find in his character; rendering him both common and reserved, violent and somber in turn, as the mood strikes him, and yet always aspiring towards an art which is at once aristocratic, formal, and objective. As Gertrude Stein has said, the soul of people does not interest Picasso very much; he is too much occupied with the body to be aware of the soul. Besides, he does not seem interested in the changing trends of thought, feeling, and imagination impinging on man today. He can believe in the eternity of what he sees, because he fails to perceive that humanity is always changing. He reduces almost everything human to a physical level, and his approach to feeling is always cold and intellectual. His painting can be sentimental, because sentimentality gives feeling an intellectual direction towards some practical action, which often startles, but does not move; conquers, but does not attract. Picasso is perhaps more, but in many ways he is less, than an artist.

No wonder that such a character had so great a success in a period when the slow natural flowing of life, which is the basis of all art, was discarded and ignored in favor of blind action. But it is also no wonder that a man of the intellectual stature and uncompromising faith in art of Picasso should, from time to time, break the bonds of his inventive fever and find surcease in contemplation. The paintings reproduced in figures 48 and 49 were done at a time when he sought to approach the ideals of classic art he had so admired during a journey to Italy. Thus a need for serenity and simplicity. *A Woman Writing* belongs to the academic tradition of painting, but Picasso was able to transform the academic scheme into a fantastic image with the full consciousness of its being a portrait of an image instead of a portrait of a woman. Both he in painting it, and we in looking at it, contemplate an image as distant from reality as it can possibly be. This distance is in the nature of an ideal, and the contemplation of that ideal is art. It is art belonging to a rarefied atmosphere, in the physical as well as in the moral sense of the word. But that is what Picasso can give us.

As we have already pointed out, the meaning of *The Red Tablecloth* is very similar to that of *A Woman Writing*. That is, Picasso attains his ideal in art by contemplating images of images which are completely detached from nature, through symbols similar to reality, and also through distorted or pseudo-geometrical forms. This aspiration towards a selected, aristocratic, serene world is Picasso's answer to the struggles of everyday life. It is an escape from the tragic implications of his sentient power into the self-satisfying world of invention—a tragic dénouement implied in the continual alternations of his success and his failure.

Another painter who thoroughly identified himself with cubism is George Braque. He contributed to the invention of cubism at least as much as Picasso did. And he proudly affirms that after the invention of cubism he never abandoned the ideal of abstract art. In fact, he never indulged in a revival of neo-classical experiences, as Picasso did. But in spite of their common ground in cubism, a work of Picasso and one of Braque bear very little resemblance to each other, because of the profound difference in the temperaments of the two artists. This, by the way, means that the personality of the artist counts for more in the artistic value of a painting than any of his theories.

Figure 50 represents a still-life, entitled *Platter of Fruit*, painted by George Braque in 1925. You will recognize in it a marble table covered by a cloth, a platter of grapes, peaches and pears, a guitar, an open album, a bottle, and a pot. The dissection and projection on the surface of the elements of things represented are evident. The leg of the table is seen on all its four sides, with one side only partially revealed. The platter also is distorted in order to show its contents. The guitar has been transformed into an almost rectangular shape.

The white cloth has become a living stream of color in order properly to frame the objects on the table. Some rectangular shapes of green marble appear both as projections of the table and as extensions of the wall in the background. All this would have no meaning at all, but for the coloring. If we, however, center our attention on the coloring, we are immediately aware that the coloring justifies the projections and distortions. The green of the rectangular-shaped marble is streaked with black and white veins, and constitutes with its rather dark tone the basis of the whole composition. The gray leg of the table has the functional purpose of supporting the table. The colors assembled on the table call for attention: white for the cloth, gray for the platter, gray-blue for the grapes, brown for the peaches, green and brown for the pears, and brown for the guitar. The intensity of the colors is very low, but the white gives them a concealed strength and a profound resonance. The whole effect is a relation between green and gray, reinforced by white and brown. All this is vague and schematic; yet even in a black-and-white reproduction one can see the infinite nuances and the sharp contrasts Braque manages to effect in his color zones. And it is precisely by this constant re-elaboration of tones that Braque succeeds in giving life to all his colors and that sometimes such life becomes mysterious and magic.

Picasso's *The Red Tablecloth* was painted in 1924, Braque's *Platter of Fruit* in 1925. They belong to the same period of taste. Yet they could hardly be more different from each other than they are. The most obvious of the differences is that Picasso's canvas is a composition of planes which have a value of their own and which are only indirectly helped

211

by colors, which here have no value of their own. On the other hand, Braque's still-life is a composition of colors which have value of their own, and which are only indirectly helped by planes and distorted forms, which in this case have no value of their own. One cannot emphasize this difference enough. If we could translate forms and colors into words, everybody would be aware that the language of Picasso belongs to another family of languages from that of Braque. This is so not only because Picasso is a Spaniard and Braque is a Frenchman, but because of the inherent difference in their characters as human beings.

Picasso is an adventurer gifted with genius. Braque is a quiet French bourgeois, who has devoted all his life to the slow development of his sensitive qualities as an artist. The greatest mystery of all is how a man of his character and temperament could become one of the foremost inventors of cubism.

Born at Argenteuil, near Paris, in 1822, of an average workaday family of wall painters, Braque has since childhood been in contact with that pictorial artisanship which has nothing to do with art, but which has much to do with the mastery of the secrets of coloring. Later, he came under the influence of the Fauves, who will be treated later on, and along with them learned to despise the imitation of nature and the images of the senses, and to seek after unknown spiritual values. However, unlike his confrères in that wild artistic movement, Braque had no desire to run after adventure for its own sake. What he was seeking was something solid, a few sound rules which would free him from what he called "improvisations after nature." He said: "Progress in art does not consist in abundance, but in the knowledge of one's limits. It is the limitation of means which determines the style, produces the new form, and encourages creative power. The limited means often give charm and strength to folk art. On the contrary, abundance brings about decadent art." And he said also: "I like the rule which corrects the emotion."[1] All this is in perfect agreement with classical principles, and is against baroque and romantic trends. And all this will explain to us what cubism meant to Braque and why he was one of the inventors of it. Coloring had no secret for him: had he loved nature, his coloring would have found all the moving lights of the universe. But he did not love nature; instead, he loved his own coloring, with all the anxiety of the owner towards his own possessions, and wanted to build up walls against the dispersals caused by nature. Certain pseudo-geometrical forms, which could be modified at will following the necessities of his coloring, were the limits he liked, and the best refuge from nature. Within these limits, Braque is not only a master; he is thus set free to create and to center all his creative power in a nuance or in a contrast of colors, as he desires. However, he never abuses his freedom to create and never abandons himself to the brilliancy of his colors. On the contrary, he is very well aware of his taking refuge within certain self-imposed artistic limits, and that, in a refuge, half-tones and low harmonies are appropriate. Hence a concentration of feeling on colors which is powerful, and rare in the history of art. Hence the magic value of his coloring—magic, because it has very little or no connection with the experience of nature and yet is as alive as nature itself.

[1] M. Raynal, *Anthologie de la Peinture en France,* 1927, p. 86.

Along with his power of concentration, his self-imposed restraint is of great value to him. It is a moral restraint, very rare in our times. He owes Picasso very much, but Picasso also is, in turn, deeply indebted to him. The evolution of his style has been perfectly coherent with his constant principles. The sphere of his research is limited but homogeneous. Such coherence is due to his moral attitude, and gives to everything he does a character of nobility and grandeur. All this can be seen in the *Platter of Fruit,* which sums up for us the essential qualities of Braque's personality.

A few years before cubism made its appearance, another trend in painting showed itself in Paris: *Fauves,* or "wild beasts," was the name given to certain painters who tried to cut themselves loose from all traditional bonds in order to look at the world with virgin eyes and reach the essence of things beyond their appearance. It can be said that cubism was a step farther, a development of Fauvism. However, an essential difference existed between Fauves and Cubists. The latter pretended to show in their paintings a scientific process and an anticipation of the geometrical essence of things. The Fauves had no such scientific aim. Their outlook was much less intellectual, and more consistent with imagination and sensibility. They stuck to coloring, as the natural way to achieve painting. Impressionists had seen in the nuances and reflections of lights and colors the effect of the appearance of nature. Fauves saw in the accord of pure tints, juxtaposed or in contrast, the effect of the absolute. Of course, pure tints could neither be adapted to academic forms nor to perspective nor to anatomy. Thus the resulting forms of

214

pure tints were distorted and abstract. But the aim of this abstraction was to exclude external nature while retaining sensibility, for sensibility and intellectual calculation were necessary to find an accord of tints. The Fauves were thus generally masters of coloring, and some of them created new chromatic harmonies which were real discoveries in the field of art.

On the other hand, their form was new, because it was adapted to the new conception of color. It was an extremely simplified form without continuity, and often without value of its own, because it depended on color. The color-form of the cubists, because of their insistence on geometry and intellectual principles, limited their possibility of expression. But the Fauves were under no such limitations in their manner of expression because through their color-form they stuck to sensibility. Their insistence on abstracting from external nature was of course intellectual. But after that moment, sensibility and imagination, left free, could, with them, convey any emotion. The detachment from external nature was thus nothing else than a striving towards something which was beyond appearance, an ideal without shape, an unknown truth. It was an approach to an unknown god, through a supposed act of mysticism. This attempt to reach an unknown superior truth through art, instead of through science — through sensibility and imagination, instead of through reasoning — was common to Fauves and Cubists alike. It was the consequence of the dissatisfaction which manifested itself at the beginning of our century, for the positivistic and materialistic thought of the second half of the nineteenth century. It was the counterpart of the disregard for nature.

If we take into consideration this common trend towards an unknown superior truth, we shall understand how Fauves and Cubists opened the way of art to the Surrealists. Surrealism is the last adventure of that advance-guard of poets and painters that still shows a certain vitality in Europe, as well as in America.

The definition of Surrealism was given by its leader, Mr. André Breton, in unmistakable terms: "It is a pure psychical automatism through which one tries by words or other means to express the real process of thinking. It is thinking which dictates, without any control by reason, and without any æsthetic or moral purpose."[1] If art is related to æsthetic purpose, action to moral purpose, and science to reasoning, it follows that a Surrealistic work is neither art, nor morals, nor science. Furthermore, as far as painting is concerned, another official surrealist writer stated that "Surrealistic painting must not be judged by artistic quality." This book is concerned with artistic quality. Therefore we could here and now dismiss Surrealistic painting from our discussion, were it not that Surrealism enhanced and emphasized some kind of feeling which belongs to the magic power of art.

Its automatism has been in painting a method for finding unexpected relations among the things of nature, and for developing ideas suggested by these things. That is, Surrealism in painting is nothing but a branch of fantastic art, the latter being a product of an imagination which is free from all ties with the rational. The imaginative quality of the Fauves and that of many painters who followed a similar path show a certain spontaneous freedom. On the other hand, Surrealists de-

[1] André Breton, *Manifeste du Surréalisme*, 1924, p. 42.

liberately set about to argue against the rational, assuming that their work was not artistic, but a new kind of knowledge. This attitude is responsible for the lack of artistic form in the majority of Surrealist painters, who by adhering strictly to the tenets of this dogma were forced to adopt a conventional academic form and to distort it without freeing themselves from it. That Surrealistic knowledge is real knowledge, may be true; but that their knowledge is not artistic knowledge, there cannot be any doubt. Thus, it would seem more profitable here to speak of certain examples of the fantastic in painting, showing a trend similar to that of Surrealism, but stopping shorter of that mysterious knowledge which is outside the field of art. Such forbearance means that those who practiced it cared less about building up a new kind of knowledge than about creating a personal form or expressing their own feelings.

The *Odalisque with Tambourine* (fig. 51) by Henri Matisse is a good example of this painter's exquisite fancy. It is the picture of a nude rendered in an academic attitude, sitting in an armchair in the middle of a room to which the richness of the colors gives a sense of luxurious disorder. A tambourine is shown in the background. And a half-open window lets the sky into the room. No representation of action, no subject matter but in the title, no specification that the naked woman is an odalisque. There is an exuding sense of oriental color in this picture, but such a color scheme could easily be duplicated in many of the villas on the French Riviera. The *Odalisque* is thus only a pretext for painting a nude. The representation of a nude in the middle of a room belongs to the discredited type of "genre painting," that is, to a chronicle of contemporary life in its everyday aspects. But it is equally true to say that the nude, the armchair, the tambourine, and so on, are simply pretexts to which Matisse pays no attention at all. His real interest in painting this picture is in the composition of colors, which should be obvious even to a novice when looking at it.

The first thing with which we are confronted, then, is the fact that Matisse, who stubbornly advocates pure colors, paints the center of his picture with neutral or almost neutral colors. The shadows of the body are gray-violet, the bright zones of the body are light brown, and some of the zones in the background are either black or gray with nuances of blue and violet. These neutral zones constitute a shadowy center around which move, as in a fantastic dance, the red of the rug, the varied greens of the armchair, the pink and the sky-blue of the veil, the green of the wall, the blue of the sky, and the red of the tambourine. The intensity of these colors is underlined by the neutrals of the center, and by their intervals and accentuations. The form is open, that is, it has no precise contours. Dabs of color seem to pervade everything in the picture, without the least regard for the forms of the objects, but at the same time obeying a necessity for balance in a fantastic pattern. There is no reason why the forms of the hands and of the feet should be mere dabs of color, no reason at all as far as the plastic form is concerned. But those dabs of color conform to a necessity of composition in colors: if hands and feet had been defined, the entire meaning of the painting would have been lost. It is true that the attitude of the woman shows the artist's perfect knowledge of drawing, and, even more, his full cognizance of the academic ideal of beauty. But in shaping the attitude of the woman the painter magically hides his academic knowledge and transforms it into a work of art. And so in modeling the woman, the only thing he seems to have cared for was the composition of those dabs of light and shadow giving the figure a certain artificial aloofness which makes her seem like an image of an image with the character of a phantasm. And since a phantasm is by nature a shadow, we must not expect to be able to count the fingers of its hands. This is the reason why Matisse stopped short in finishing hands and feet.

One does not see phantasms in nature. Nor does one see colors as intense as those which dance around the phantasm in the picture. Here is the justification of the form of Matisse, and here too the perfect balance of the neutral and the intense colors in the picture. Once he has detached himself from reality and entered the pure world of fancy, Matisse is able to maintain as perfect a coherence with shadows as with dabs of bright color.

Matisse introduces us to a fabulous realm, where richness, luxury, and ideal beauty are so tempered with artistic equilibrium, balance, tact, finesse, natural ease, that the contemplation of his work is an enchantment. The mystery of his work is veiled by the natural ease of his creative power, but remains, underneath, as a suggestion that everything in the picture is beyond the realm of reality.

Henri Matisse was born in 1869, devoted himself to art in 1892, and became the leader of the Fauves in 1905. He never accepted the method of Cubism, living on to enjoy the revival of Fauvism which took place in Paris in 1929, of which he still remains easily the outstanding representative.

He once said: "I express the space and the objects placed there as naturally as though I had only the sea and the sky before me, that is to say, the simplest things in the world. So, to explain the unity realized in my picture, however complex it may be, is not difficult for me, because it comes to me naturally. I think only about rendering my emotion. Very often, an artist's difficulty lies in his not taking into consideration the quality of his emotion, and in allowing his reasoning to misguide this emotion. He should use his reasoning only for control."[1]

This is a happy statement of the conscious artistic process. It is difficult to find a clearer one coming from an artist's mind. Creation must be natural, according to the quality of one's emotion, without interference by reason, which may easily misguide it, and which should act only as control of the emotion after the process of creation has ended. This is the true process of any artist who succeeds in reaching his goal. Because his art is fantastic, such a conscious process is especially interesting in Matisse, whose ability to control the subtle workings of his own clear mind, as though he were a spectator looking on, helps him greatly in freeing himself from the shackles of reasoning and consciousness during the period of creation, and in abandoning himself to imagination and fancy. The workings of his imagination seem to begin after Matisse's reasoning has cleared the ground of the habit of thinking, which means everyday practical thinking. And it is precisely through such a dialectic process that his imag-

[1]This, and the following quotations from Matisse, are taken from *La Grande Revue,* December, 1908, and *L'Intransigéant,* January 14–22, 1929.

ination becomes free and is able to convey emotion. Thus, in his best works, such a process is not an arbitrary one, but rather a creative one.

Matisse's interest in human life is narrow. No religious, no social, no dramatic feeling can be found in him. But he makes up for this narrowness by his purity. Within his own world, made of enchanting colors and patterns, his fancy has no limits. Everywhere his fancy reaches, there is creation. And this is why he does go so far into this unknown world of fancy.

The third dimension in Matisse's paintings is never totally absent; but because colors and patterns can very well exist without a third dimension, he cares very little for it. Many critics have alluded to this relative lack of a third dimension as a shortcoming of the artist. But this is only a shortcoming of the critics. The third dimension is a source of art, but the surface too is a source of art. If Matisse had emphasized the third dimension more, as he did in a few paintings, his coherence would have diminished and his art would not have been realized at its best. Only if one accepts the world of enchanting colors and patterns, can he understand that perfection which is Matisse's.

Enchantment of colors and patterns is at once the form and the content of Matisse's art. But for the purpose of analysis it is possible to consider his form and his content separately, and to ask the painter himself for an indication of them.

He wrote: "Suppose I set out to paint an interior: I have before me a cupboard; it gives me a sensation of bright red and I put down a red which satisfies me; immediately a relation is established between this red and the white of the canvas. If I put a green near the red, if I paint in a yellow floor, there must still be between this green, this yellow and the white of the canvas a relation that will be satisfactory to me. But these several tones mutually weaken one another. It is necessary, therefore, that the various elements that I use be so balanced that they do not destroy one another. . . . A new combination of colors will succeed the first one and will give more completely my interpretation. I am forced to transpose until finally my picture may seem completely changed when, after successive modifications, the red has succeeded the green as the dominant color." This is a perfect description of the process which transforms a physical sensation into an imaginative painting, that is, into an original creation of Matisse's own form of colors.

Concerning his content, Matisse wrote: "What I dream of is an art of balance, of purity and serenity devoid of troubling or depressing subject matter, an art which might be for every mental worker, be he a business man or writer, like an appeasing influence, like a mental soother, something like a good armchair in which to rest from physical fatigue." Is it shocking to reduce the ideal of art to an armchair? The courage of Matisse's sincerity here should be praised rather than condemned. It throws a clear light on his art and on art in general. We must judge his art within the limits of his ideal, since his sincerity in determining this ideal means the integration of that perfect choice of motifs, adapted to form and hence revealed by his form, which is the basis of his grandeur as an artist.

Figure 52 reproduces a watercolor — *Pertaining to Stoning-*

ton Harbor, Maine, painted by John Marin in 1926. To understand this work, it is important to bear in mind the trend called "Fantastic Art," that is, Fauvism and Surrealism. It is true that since John Marin is an American painter, deeply rooted in American soil and highly conscious of its attitude to life, no one has yet connected him with the modern trends of French painting. It is also true that Marin stated that his pictures "are conservative and belong to convention." But this means only that, like all the foremost revolutionists in art, Marin is a revolutionist without knowing it. What we see in figure 52 is a small harbor with a big sailboat. Immediately we realize that the relationship between the sailboat and the harbor is an unnatural one: it is a relationship born of affection, and not of perspective. In the background are some village houses barely sketched in, one of which looks very much like a monumental romanesque cathedral. The actual house which served as a model for the one represented in the picture was, no doubt, a rather poor one, but Marin loved it and transformed it. Farther off in the background, we see also some mountains which are barely suggested. However, the formal accord existing among the forms of the sailboat, the houses, and the mountains has a charm all its own, a charm compounded of balance and of structure which is intensely alive.

Marin's ideal is one of coordination, of balance, and of structure. The lively intensity of the picture reflects Marin's own intensity of feeling, rather than his will. To coordinate the structure of his vision (sailboat, houses, mountains) with the other parts of his picture, Marin resorted to projections. The use of projections is, as we have seen, typical of Cubism. Marin's projections are as abstract as those of the Cubists, but their function is different, because they serve to complete the expression of a central emotion which is perfectly real. A zone in the upper right corner has a magical suggestion. And the corresponding zones in the lower part of the painting are just as abstract, and have the function of uniting the whole, of balancing it, and of giving the vision a constant rhythm. The result is that pattern and structure are so well interwoven that every element is developed both on surface and in depth. An object is created which has its own life, its own charm. The objectivity and independence of the picture, dreamed of by Fauves and Cubists, is here realized with the touch of magic so dear to the Surrealists. But at the same time we find here the expression of an emotion, of an attachment to a sailboat and to some houses, and of an enthusiasm for a natural vision which is thoroughly personal. Such expression, realized through the nervous play of light and shade, is concentrated in the sailboat and houses. All the rest—mountains, sea water, and projections—is mere structural frame for the central motif. The colors of the sailboat and the houses are white and gray, that of the water is dark blue, those of the mountains nuances of lighter blue, with some splashes of brown in the foreground. The color scheme could not be simpler. The dark tones of blue and brown help to focus the qualities of the white and gray, which, in turn, reveal a frame in depth which is the structural frame of the picture. Thus, the resulting unity of form and color is perfect.

John Marin was born in Rutherford, New Jersey, in 1870. He studied art in Philadelphia and New York, where for a short time he became a free-lance architect. In 1905 he went to Paris, where he lived, with the exception of a few visits home, until 1911. During this European period, his etchings showed the influence of Whistler, while his oil paintings showed that of Monet. But after 1908 his watercolors became absolutely personal, and through the support of Alfred Stieglitz brought him a measure of renown which is still widely current even today.

Marin has painted oils as good as his watercolors. But most of his artistic production was done in watercolors, and many critics have thought it a shortcoming in the artist. This is sheer nonsense. A watercolor by Cézanne is not one whit the less art than one of his oils. A poem with short lines is not one jot the less art than a poem with long lines. And just as a certain technique determines certain characteristics of a work of art, so a certain type of vision adapted to watercolor technique cannot be realized in oil without suffering in its artistic quality. But, if through an oil technique an artist achieves certain artistic qualities that he cannot achieve through the use of watercolor, the contrary is also true, that through the use of watercolor he may attain a certain lightness, rapidity, and delicacy in expression that he cannot possibly attain through oil painting. One might say that the craftsmanship in oil is more elaborate than the craftsmanship in watercolor, but it is time to distinguish between craftsmanship and art.

Marin has painted much out of doors. But since 1919 he has preferred to elaborate his motifs indoors where, he said, "I can do better, visualizing what I have experienced through my eyes." He was too conscientious, however, to ignore na-

225

ture. "I don't paint rocks, trees, houses, and all things seen, I paint an inner vision. Rubbish. If you have an intense love and feeling towards these things, you'll try your dam'dest to put on paper or canvas that thing. You can transpose, you can play with and on your material, but when you are finished, that's got to have the roots of that thing in it and no other thing."[1] By such principles, Marin avoided the abstraction of sentiment from life and nature, appropriate to Cubism, and maintained his relation, even when indirect, with his natural vision. What he opposed was this: "Reason and knowledge are the things we have to combat, they are always fighting sight. The thing seems to be to know how we see, not to let our knowing how the thing is, to conflict." And what he despised was eclecticism, "A sort of Pseudo Romantic Chaldean Persian Grecian Roman Italian French German combination vision, an Abstract Concreteness, a monumental memory of other things."

Marin expressed his structural ideal in the following way: "To get to my picture . . . I must for myself insist that, when finished, that is when all its parts are in place and are working, that now it has become an object and will therefore have its boundaries as definite as — that the prow, the stern, the sides and bottom, bound a boat."

Marin's sense of dynamics was based on the principle of *weights and balances:* "As my body exerts a downward pressure on the floor, the floor in turn exerts an upward pressure on my body; too, the pressure of the air against my body —

---

[1]This, and the following quotations of Marin's ideas, are taken from *Letters of John Marin,* New York, privately printed for An American Place, 1931 (without numbered pages).

my body against the air — all this I have to recognize when building the picture."

Such dynamics are rooted in the spontaneous reactions of the artist to, for instance, the sight of New York skyscrapers or Maine sunsets. "It is this *moving of me* that I try to express, so that I may recall the spell I have been under and behold the expression of the different emotions that have been called into being."

A shy, retiring man, Marin has always loved "houses, islands, and boats." His desire has always been to paint the things he loved, and to dedicate to the glory of these things his boundless imagination. He didn't "need to paint master-pieces and be conceited," to feel that he had accomplished something worthwhile in his painting. So that a correspondence exists in him between dynamics and love, as well as between balance and modesty. And it is precisely this moral quality of his vision, this emotional content of his imagination, which is responsible for the enchantment of his art.

While speaking of Matisse and Marin we tried to explain why they ought to be considered as exponents of Fantastic Art, even if they themselves never thought of having anything to do with Surrealism. Chagall, on the other hand, has been considered by official Surrealists as one of their forerunners, one who is sometimes within the limits of Surrealism and sometimes beyond it.

The painting reproduced here (fig. 53) has obvious Surrealistic elements in it, but also goes beyond mere Surrealism. It represents *The Martyr* and was painted in 1940, with an obvious reference to the martyrdom of Jewish people in

Poland and other countries of Eastern Europe. Its aim is thus not fantastic, but historical, because it represents a veri-similar event of the present war; and it is religiously symbolic because the dead Jew tied to the pile is spiritually related to the crucified Christ, the pile representing a symbolic cross. Nevertheless, the fantastic element does exist in this picture in the way it is conceived. And, in keeping with the distinction made at the beginning of this book, the subject matter is historical and symbolical, but the content is fantastic.

The symbolic importance of the figures is indicated by their physical proportions; the martyr, intended to exert the strongest pull on our emotion, is the largest; next in importance and size comes the woman crying at the feet of the martyr; followed by the other figures whose size and distance from the foreground are determined by the degree of their participation in the drama, and not by their position in the picture. The same order of importance applies also to the symbolic character of the animals; one being a non-existent animal, half-cow and half-woman; the other a bird resembling a cock.

The plastic form of the human figures in this picture is not intended to render their objective reality, but is subordinated to colors and is simplified in order to constitute zones of color-variations. It is the yellow of the body of the martyr, underlined by the black-and-white shirt, which conveys the feeling of the tragedy represented in the picture. It is the pink of the veil and of the blouse worn by the woman at the foot of the pile, and the blue, orange, and green stripes of her gown which suggest a sweet, resigned, melancholic sorrow. Contrasting with this note of resignation is the green

228

garb and orange face of the violin player and the shining sky-blue and pink colors of the violin suggesting an escape from tragedy. And it is the dark blue, forming the group of the mother and child, which accentuates the expression of fear and despair in the attitude and form of the figures. All these colors are, in other words, the protagonists of the drama enacted in the picture against the neutral gray of a village over which hangs the thick pall of the heavy brown smoke of the destroying fire. Only at the top of the canvas is the sky suggested by a thin zone of blue and white.

There are, moreover, in this picture some peculiarities of form which serve as accompaniment and commentary on the tragedy. The smoke rising above the houses assumes a vague human form, to accentuate the meaning of human cruelty and of impending destruction. The houses seem to tremble as though rocked by an earthquake. A leg of the fantastic animal ends in a woman holding a candlestick. A man is shown jumping headlong out of a window preceded by his chair. And as final fantastic gesture, the top of the head of the violin player is abolished altogether.

The unity of the composition is due to contrast. The plane on which the figures are arranged is convex. The background, on the contrary, suggests empty space in depth. This means that the painter conceived his picture in two consecutive moments: first, the figures dominating the whole, and then, the background as a later commentary. However, the figures must also have been conceived separately, with the violin player, the mother and child and the animals, seen as episodes connected with the main theme spiritually only, not visually. And the unity of the martyr and the woman crying

229

is almost as loosely conceived and rendered, depending, as it does, on style, on a common undulating line.

Chagall's expression of tragedy in *The Martyr* is, no doubt, a very powerful one, but it is not dependent on action at all. It is the colors as well as the forms of the picture which express the artist's feeling by broken, discordant glares. It is this broken continuity which characterizes the style of Chagall, which is responsible for his withdrawal from the world of reality, and which constitutes his poetry of the fantastic. And, if without unity of expression there is no art, what, then, is the unity of this broken continuity?

Marc Chagall was born in Vitebsk, Russia, in 1887, of poor Jewish parents. The pity he feels for the misery of his people and for domestic animals has been the basic sentiment of his life. Along with that feeling, the mystery of popular legends also attracted him. His people and animals constitute his connection with reality, and his necessity to stick to the things of earth. At the same time, the legends cherished during his childhood and a natural trend towards unbridled fancy obliged him to detach himself from reality. Narrow, fragmentary realism and unbridled fancy are characteristic of popular art and poetry. To overcome this characteristic of popular art in his own work it was necessary to strike a balance between his realism and his fancy. Chagall found this balance in Paris, where he arrived in 1910, when his approach to French art was that of a rebel against both Impressionism and Cubism. Nevertheless, and perhaps in spite of himself, he learned a great deal from both movements. Besides the geometric essence of a simplified form, he learned how to express himself through coloring; he learned the possibilities of its nuances and contrasts; and the construction of forms conceived to serve coloring. But both impressionistic and cubistic conceptions of art appeared to him too tied to the physical world to give sufficient scope to his art. He said it was necessary to transform nature not only materially from the outside, but also ideologically from the inside, without fear of what has been called *literary* in painting. What Chagall learned in Paris was not only a more perfect painting technique, but also a new boldness in following his own way. A new, essential element in his art, he acquired when he went back to Russia in 1914: it was love, the sweetness of living, after so many years of misery and intellectual trial — and happiness, of which he now speaks as of a lost paradise.

If we now try to find a relation between all these elements in his life we may consider *The Martyr* a summary of it. The pity he has always felt for his people has become, because of the present war, a catastrophic vision of all mankind where a crucified man appears gigantic against the background of a crumbling village scorched by fire and earthquake. But instead of concentrating on the tragedy, Chagall indulges himself in his popular humorous stories. Fantastic beasts, as well as mankind itself, have now become co-protagonists in the tragedy, as the leg of the cow, metamorphosed into the symbolic Jewish candlestick, shows — as the popular song bursting forth from the violin of the headless player, as the bearded man poring over the Bible for an explanation of the tragedy, and as the mother driven by fear and grief eloquently confirm. Furthermore, the grace of a woman in her sweet, melancholic and resigned sorrow is always present

231

in the work of Chagall, as a delicate flower surviving in a cruel, arid desert.

This sweetness is the clue to the art of Chagall. He has been and is still very much the rebel in art; but he is still, too, one of the sweetest, gentlest, and most frightened of men on earth. Yet, in spite of his timidity, he is often surprisingly capable of bursts of the most daring flights of pure fancy. All his contradictions appear simultaneously on his canvases, and because of their simultaneity, the unity of his work is to be found in a certain apparent discord — in a certain broken continuity — between the various elements and the whole. Never has fancy been more unbridled and, at the same time, more full of the most varied nuances of sentiment than in Chagall's work. And as his vision cannot find its unity of expression in physical proportions in space, or in plastic form, it finds it in something which is a more fluent and changing medium, in his glamorous coloring.

Conclusion

THE AIM of this book has been to introduce the reader to certain paintings which the author has deemed, for one reason or another, worthy of the reader's attention — if in some few cases only as a means of negative contrast — in order that the reader's critical experience might be enriched thereby.

The author could not offer him in the foregoing pages a system of painting or a science of art, since he does not believe that a science of art is possible, because painting as a work of art is not a material thing, where one could work with instruments, experiments, and reasoning, as a scientist does. Kant said that there is no science of art, but only criticism of art. And he is still right.

A painter works with his sight, his feeling, and his imagination. All the rules of science — for example, that of perspective — or of morals, religion, or philosophy, applied to the sight, feeling, and imagination of a painter have resulted in nonsense. In short, there is no rule and there can be none for a creative painter. Each painter, if he is a real artist, creates his own rule, which is good for him, but which is generally bad for all other painters.

To learn, and know, how to look at a painting does not mean to be bound by any rule, but to be free of all rules. And to be free of all rules is not so easy as it seems at first. In fact, the rules exist, some are a couple of thousand years old. They are taught in all schools; we learn them from childhood, and as every one knows, we, as creatures of habit, do not easily discard anything we have gone to the trouble of learning laboriously.

Socrates said that the acme of wisdom is to know that we know nothing. A great deal of wisdom is necessary indeed to approach painting with an open mind. Wisdom is always accompanied by a certain sense of humility. The tendency of so many people to tell a painter what he must paint and how he must paint his pictures is the surest way of understanding nothing of his work. If we wish to understand a poem by Baudelaire, the first thing we ought to do is to learn the French language. But even this is not enough. We ought also to learn that personal language which is Baudelaire's, if we want to understand him. The painter too has his own language, which is constituted of a personal fusion of lines, forms, and colors. This language we have to learn, and to see why it is similar to or different from the language of all other painters. A proper understanding of the fusion of many lines, forms, and colors is necessary if we wish to understand even one picture. Such understanding is known as culture in painting. Similarly, to have read many good poems is called culture in poetry. This book has attempted to offer the reader an approach to about fifty paintings, with the purpose of serving as a primer of culture in painting. But culture is never contained in or acquired from a primer. A primer is merely a springboard, a first step on the long road to acquiring a culture.

Yet as we have pointed out at the beginning of this book, even culture is not enough for deciding whether a panel or a canvas covered by colors and forms is, or is not, a work of art. Such decision or judgment is the first and ultimate step in art criticism. That is, by understanding what a painter has expressed, the critic must judge whether such expression is within or outside the realm of art. It is in arriving at this judgment that culture in painting is not enough. Such culture can tell us whether the expression is similar to or different from that of other paintings. But to consider a painting, or many paintings, a standard of measure for all paintings means to fail to recognize any new standard set up by a new artistic personality, new either to our culture or new because born in our day. Where culture in painting is not enough, we must perforce have recourse to the whole culture of man, which means that in order to judge whether a painting is, or is not, a work of art, one ought to have at least an inkling of all human activities before deciding whether, instead of being a work of art, it is not a scientific demonstration, a moral or religious sermon, or a practical program for political, social, or economic action, disguised as art.

The ideal would be to have at our disposal a clear definition of art, and to check our interpretation of a single painting with that definition of art, in order to see whether such a painting meets the requirements of the definition. But art is a human activity, and every human activity is very complex. Therefore, the reader must not be surprised if we cannot produce, *ipso facto,* a ready definition of art. A scientist is not required to pull out of his hat, as a magician does, a ready-made definition of science, or a philosopher a definition of philosophy. The best the author can do here is to suggest a reading of the *Æsthetics* of Benedetto Croce and *Art as Experience* by John Dewey, which, notwithstanding their

235

many differences, complement each other, and are perhaps the most important books on æsthetics written in our time.

Still better would it be to compare these two modern books on æsthetics with two of the most glorious ones of the past — *The Critique of Judgment* by Immanuel Kant and the *Philosophy of Art* by George Hegel.

What has been offered in the foregoing pages is not a formal treatise on æsthetics but a concrete experience in artistic judgment, based not only on the ideas of Croce and of Dewey, of Kant and of Hegel, but also on many ideas drawn from the history of æsthetics and the history of criticism. The conclusion of that experience is that only the reconstruction of the personality of the painter can suggest to us whether he is a real artist, or whether, hidden under color and form and technique, he has an economic, political, religious, or other similar extra-artistic axe to grind.

In so doing, one does not ignore the definition of art, but finds it not in an abstract formula but in a living reality. Such a method is certainly not a scientific one, if we consider science in the physical sense. It is a historical method, and the best one, we believe, for critical purposes.

In the body of this book, we have sought to distinguish two moments in the approach to a painting: the moment of interpretation, and the moment of judgment. Such a distinction is useful for practical purposes, but in essence it is evident that they ultimately combine in one. When we read a poem, for example, we may enjoy one passage more than another, or disapprove of still another altogether, at the very moment we reach an understanding of them, suspending our judgment on them until we have realized the meaning of the

236

whole poem, and bestowing or withholding our praise as the case may be.

The same thing applies to painting. The first impression of a picture is quite vague, and it is only after an analysis of all its components that we may really understand the meaning of each of them and of the picture as a whole. But we cannot fully appreciate that meaning unless we ourselves have first been emotionally moved, by attraction or repulsion, and without our feeling and imagination guiding us in praise or disapproval. That is, our interpretation cannot be the "factual" interpretation the so-called scientists of art are seeking.

Even a single example will, we believe, suffice to clarify this point. Let us suppose you are looking at a painting representing Venus. The painter's aim may have been to portray ideal beauty or the object of his earthly love. If we believe that the painting's content is love, then our interpretation will be based upon our feeling of its being a spontaneous expression of love or an exhibition of meretricious sensuality. Therefore, in accordance with this feeling, we will judge it as a work of art or as a pornographic act at the very moment we realize the nature of the love which is the content of that painting. Lines, forms, and colors will then appear to us so strictly interwoven with the nature of that love that our appreciation or disapproval of them will follow as a natural consequence.

In other words, we ourselves would be making the history of all the elements included in a painting, and the criticism of it as a whole, its synthesis, and its result. History and criticism react on each other constantly, so that without a correct interpretation of the psychological factors involved our criticism will fail, but also without the constant intervention of our artistic feeling our interpretation will be false.

Thus the best way of looking at a painting is to strive to understand, and thus appreciate, the intimate relationship existing between the lines, forms, and colors we see in the picture and the feeling and the imagination of the artist which we do not see but which we can sense and reconstruct by or through our feeling and imagination. So that, finally, the analysis of a painting reveals not only the artistic activity of the painter, but also the whole of his human activity.

Without technique no painting would be possible. But with technique alone we should have no art. Technique is a practical activity, a means to an end, the end being to achieve art. Technique is only an element, not the whole of art. Thus one cannot judge a work of art on the basis of its technique. Furthermore, any technique, when suited to the artist, is good enough for achieving a work of art. Thus, a critic should not rate one technique higher than another. A prejudice still rooted in many people is, for example, that Giotto had a more imperfect technique than Raphael. It is fitting and proper therefore to state here that Giotto's technique is different from, but not inferior to, that of any one else. It is indeed foolish to measure the technique of Giotto by that of any other painter. The sole purpose of Giotto's technique was to realize Giotto's art. Giotto's art being perfect, his technique must also be perfect. For the same reason, it is not true that Cézanne had less of a mastery of drawing technique than Raphael: Cézanne's drawing technique was perfectly suited to his conception of reflections of tones. If Cézanne had indulged in academic drawing, he would never

238

have found that personal technique through which he was able to realize his masterpieces. Thus an artistic judgment must not be indifferent to technique, since it must decide whether or not the technique used by an artist is adapted to his vision, feeling, and imagination. But what the critic must avoid is to consider a given technique superior or inferior to any other. The perfection or the shortcoming of a technique is always related to the personality of the artist who uses it, and to nobody else.

This point must be emphasized because of the confusion manifested on this aspect of painting by many art critics. The senseless hubbub of recent years about the superiority of fresco over oil painting was one of the worst manifestations of this confusion. We have seen that in the sixteenth century Michelangelo found artistic perfection through fresco painting, and Titian through oil painting. No doubt Michelangelo found in fresco the best technique for his plastic vision, a vision most closely akin to marble sculpture; but Titian needed oil technique to realize his pictorial vision. As plastic vision is not superior to pictorial vision, fresco is not superior to oil. As an artist, John Marin has not yet been recognized at his real value because he generally paints watercolors instead of oils. It is ridiculous to think that art must depend on oil or water, like a salad dressing. When John Marin uses watercolor technique, he does so because that medium gives him a freer scope for his imagination. And let us not forget to take into account that an artist is a serious person, with serious work to do, who should not have to be bothered with futilities or malice. In technique nothing is absolute: all is relative to the painter who uses it and to nobody else.

There is a good and a bad technique. The good one is that which is appropriate to the artist's vision and ideal. The bad one is that which overwhelms the artist's vision and ideal. This happens when the painter prefers to be a technician, a virtuoso, rather than an artist. Meissonier and Bouguereau are good examples of such failure.

Very likely no painter ever lived who did not hold to some theory or other, since the contribution of intellect to painting is a necessary condition of art. But like technique, a theory is either good or bad only insofar as it is of help or hindrance to the free expression of feeling and the free development of the imagination. The theory of Piero della Francesca was spatial order; that of Renoir was irregularity. Their theories could not be more remote from each other. Yet they proved to have been helpful to Piero della Francesca and to Renoir in creating their masterpieces. On the other hand, the theory of Cubism did not prove to be so helpful to Picasso, since it is obvious that he did his best things when he dispensed with Cubism. One can say that Renoir and Piero della Francesca realized their art within the limits of their theories, and that Picasso realized his in spite of his theory.

The ideal of irregularity helped Renoir in the development of his imagination. He followed his sensibility with the clear consciousness that he ought to be true to it without limits. Being gifted with a very lively imagination, he created images in accordance with his sensibility.

On the other hand, no doubt the theory of Piero della Francesca was a limitation to the freedom of his imagination. But regular geometric forms coordinated in perspective had in his mind, and in that of his contemporaries, something of the divine — that is, they were not regular forms regarded with the cool mind of a mathematician, but adored in the mood of a faithful follower. Because of that mood, regular forms lost their scientific character and became artistic forms.

The case of Picasso is quite different. The fact that he contributed to the invention of Cubism, used it, then abandoned it, then resumed it, shows that it was for him not an ideal, deeply rooted in his soul, but an experiment. Besides, as the quoted passage from Apollinaire's manifesto on Cubism shows, the approach to Cubism was anything but artistic. These two facts combined lead us to believe that Picasso's imagination followed its own path, in casual adherence or in opposition to his theory.

The danger of theory in art is similar to the danger of technique. When an artist is so tied to his theory that it prevents his imagination from working freely and his sensibility from being true to itself, then his painting is either a failure or it is imperfect. The paintings of Ingres or of Puvis de Chavannes, as analyzed in the body of this book, are good examples of such shortcomings.

The problem of theory in art is connected with the problem of knowledge. There is no doubt that art contributes to the knowledge of mankind. If not, art would be only a useless play. But the difficulty is to state what kind of knowledge it is. It is different from both scientific knowledge and mystic knowledge. Scientific knowledge deals with types and categories, with generalizations seeking to approach universal truth. Mystic knowledge jumps at universal truth without bothering about verification of its process. Artistic knowledge is essentially individual, but implies the universal. A landscape painting portrays a few fragments of the world, a tree, a river, a mountain. But such fragments are painted in accordance with the style of the painter, which includes the ideal of artistic activity which, in turn, belongs to the universal and the infinite. Thus in that landscape painting there is a fragmentary individual bit of earth and the universal ideal of the painter. The relation between the individual and the universal is, thus, the knowledge offered by art. That we may find in some reflections in water the eternal song of light and shade is a revelation which painting can make.

The conscious offering of a definite knowledge through a painting can make its artistic result more profound, but it can also be an obstacle to the realization of a work of art. If the imagination of the painter is pushed to the point of classifying knowledge according to type, category, or generality in competition with science, the picture will lose both its individual character and its universal implication. On the other hand, if the imagination of the artist in its mystic fervor foregoes any individual knowledge, his work will be lost in what cannot be expressed — in the ineffable. The exigency of finding in a painting the relationship between an individual meaning and a universal implication must be kept in mind by any art criticism.

The difference in the artistic quality of the man and the woman in *À la Mie* by Toulouse-Lautrec (fig. 30) can be explained by such exigency, the man being individualized to such an extent that he lacks style. This cannot be said of the woman. On the other hand, the lack of any individual realization in Puvis de Chavannes' *Vision of the Antique* (fig. 14) reveals the emptiness of his mysticism

242

and a weakness of imagination which is artistic weakness.

Every painting that is a work of art has also a moral or religious feeling. This does not mean that it must support any particular moral theory or religion. The very opposite is true: a work to be art must go beyond any moral or religious credo. But a work of art must participate in that aspiration towards a universal harmony which is typical of moral or religious feelings. If not, art loses that universal implication which is necessary to its character as art, as we have pointed out in the foregoing pages. The danger of introducing moral or religious laws into art lies precisely in the fact that they are laws and not that they are moral or religious. The application of or adherence to any law hinders that spontaneity of creation which is the essential condition of art. Even when evincing a moral or religious purpose, paintings lacking in spontaneity of creation are usually resented as immoral.

The case of Millet is typical. As we have seen, he was morally and socially right, and he was sincere. But the expression of his ideal, though morally and socially right, was pervaded by a will to convince that has nothing to do with art. And because of that will to convince he lost the spontaneity of creation. Kant indicated something similar when he affirmed that disinterestedness was essential to art. Even a moral interest, if it prevails over the artist's freedom of imagination, hinders the work of art. The idea of spontaneity represents quite well that moment of the artistic process when all the technical, intellectual, or moral interests are forgotten, and the artist goes on producing like a flowering tree.

This also explains why every real artist appears to be a primitive. Primitive people are people whose imagination ignores thought, doubt, and reasoning, and whose social behavior disregards organized conventions. So, a real painter, even the most civilized, at a certain moment during his creative process must destroy in himself thought, doubt, reasoning, and organized conventions. And in order to create he must become primitive. In this sense, of course, Rembrandt or Cézanne is as primitive as Giotto or Berlinghieri.

The danger for a painter is that of becoming primitivistic, not primitive; that is, of imitating the stylistic manner of some ancient or not quite thoroughly civilized painter. Of course, the aim of the primitivists is to cheat the observer, that is, to let him believe that their forms are spontaneous rather than consciously and wilfully imitated. Their artistic attitude is thus an immoral one. Again, to cite Puvis de Chavannes, his *Vision of the Antique* is a good example of the spurious primitive — the primitivistic.

Something of reality and of the ideal are necessary to a work of art. But what is reality in a painting? Let us take a painting representing a tree. It is not the tree represented which is the reality in the painting, but the image of the tree. That is, the painter sees a tree in nature: he sees it luminous or shadowy, strong or frail, large or small, sound and at peace, or distorted and tormented by storms. These or similar qualities of the tree will be evident in the painted image of the tree — if the painting is a real work of art. And these are precisely those qualities which constitute the reality of the pictorial image. Thus the reality in a painting is not the thing in nature in itself but the kind of approach the artist has made to the thing in nature. For reality in painting is not objective; it is subjective. If we do not find artistic reality in a cubistic painting, it is not because we do not see there a tree or a mountain as we see them in nature, but because the painter's language utterly fails to communicate to us the way the painter saw or felt the thing. And we conclude that in that painting there is no content.

Reality in painting identifies itself with the content of the painting. As we have already noted, content and form must be fused in a work to be art. But we may speak of content as distinguished from form for the practical purpose of classification. A painter sees a tree, feels its majesty, imagines its relation to the surrounding world, rejoices at the play of light and shadow on it. All this, and much else, are the content as well as the reality of his painting.

Then he elaborates his form in accordance with his ideal. We have already spoken of his ideals of technique, of science, of morals, and of religion. But there are many other types of ideal for a painter. One dreams of plastic form, another of pictorial form. One sticks to structure, another to pattern. One prefers proportions and statics, another anatomy and movement. One enjoys a composition on the surface, another a composition in depth. One wants to coordinate the components of his picture, another to subordinate all to one dominating component. One seeks relief through chiaroscuro, and another volumes through colors and their tonality. One loves intense colors, another colors subdued by the effect of light and shade. One wants to give his forms a close, accurate finish, another believes that a certain degree of loose, open finish is better for the effect of the whole. Furthermore, some painters long for beauty, physical or moral; others for grace, and still others for the sublime, the picturesque, and so on.

245

All these are ideals in painting, all condition the form of each painting. And here we must emphasize that while all these ideals may be useful in achieving an artistic form, no one of them is better or worse than any other. In fact, all depend on the creative power of the artist for their realization. Thus, the only standard for their appreciation is the personality of the artist. Those ideals which have been realized in a work of art, must be admired; others must be ignored. Any of them may be good for one painter and bad for all others.

We have seen many instances of this fact. The ideal of beauty which prompted Raphael's masterpieces, led Bouguereau into his blunders. The ideal of illustration which supported the genius of Goya, destroyed the talent of Meissonier. We love in Simone Martini the ideal of the finished, as we love in Constable the ideal of the unfinished. We love in Botticelli the ideal of grace, and in Pollaiuolo the ideal of violence. We love in Masaccio or in Michelangelo the plastic form, as we love in Rembrandt or in Cézanne the pictorial form.

Every painter has his own ideal which will guide us towards an understanding of his painting. But no particular one of them must be allowed to foster any prejudice in us or to dominate our judgment at the expense of all others.

The object of praise or disapproval is neither the reality nor the content, the ideal nor the form, of the painting. What should be the object of our concern is the personality of the painter—his ability in expressing any content, provided it be his own content, through any form, provided it be his own form.

246

CONCLUSION

The reconstruction of the personality of the artist will show us whether he is spontaneous or artificial, whether he expresses his content without overemphasizing naturalistic detail, whether he absorbs in his style all the elements of his painting and, finally, whether he shows that coherence of the imagination which in art is the quality parallel to logic in science.

The principal aim of this book has been to stress the relativity of all the components of any painting. They are subject to the arbitrary preferences of individuals, of fashions, and of civilizations. They are always changing, and they constitute what since the eighteenth century has been called taste.

It is only by reducing all the components of a work of art to the condition of relativity, that we can understand what is absolute in art—which is the personality of the artist. Art can be found only in the individual, but it is universal art we find in him. The microcosm contains the macrocosm. So that in any work of art is contained the essence of all art. And this is the essential of all art: its ability to identify the individual with the universal.

This theory of the relative value of all the components of a work of art is the only one which can discover the absolute value of art, as it is revealed in the ensemble of the work itself. And it is that ensemble which constitutes the personality of the artist.

To analyze all the components is a necessary part of art criticism, but it is also necessary to look beyond what one sees—to look with the eyes of the mind into the painter's soul.

If this book should induce any one to do this, its purpose will have been fulfilled.

Index